ARROWHEA

MW00648939

Ultimate Guide

to

Indian Artifact Hunting

by William Bauer

Edited by J. Kristi Hood

[handwritten marginalia:] field after a rain → rivers: sand bars after big flood → : same spot after every flood → Topo : find old rivers

Copyright William Bauer
Published May 2013
All rights reserved.

Email: willy@wheretofindarrowheads.com

Special Thanks to Sean Melton,
a true EXPERT ARROWHEAD HUNTER.

Table of Contents

INTRODUCTION
Power of the Finding

Finding Indian artifacts is a powerful experience. First you feel the thrill of discovering buried treasure. Then you realize what you found is thousands of years old. You hold in your hand a physical connection to the past, present, and future. History is an abstract concept. When you find an arrowhead, the abstract becomes concrete. For me, finding artifacts is a religious experience. An arrowhead is physical proof of the continuity of mankind. Every time I find an arrowhead I see the face of God. One hunter I know tattoos his best finds on his back, like tally marks on a weapon. Possession of artifacts is fleeting. In the end, you can't take them with you, and they will be here long after you are gone. Finding your own arrowheads is where the magic lives. It's not about owning rocks. It's about FINDING them.

Beginners find artifacts by accident, or because someone told them where to look. Many people want to find arrowheads, but the steep learning curve guarantees most would-be hunters end up as buyers instead. It was two years before I found anything good on my own. During these first years I hunted with many experienced people, learning their tools and techniques. In the process of learning from many teachers, I realized that each had only part of the picture. I was often given inaccurate and conflicting advice. In this early phase I was finding arrowheads accidentally and not very often, in spite of trying very, very hard.

Every old-time artifact hunter will tell you "30 years ago you could bring home 10 arrowheads a day, but it's not like that anymore." The few books available are written by the same people who tell you productive arrowhead hunting is a thing of the past. Those who came before were operating in a different time when artifacts and landowner permission were easy to come by. Consequently there is no modern school of artifact hunting. How would one go about finding arrowheads TODAY and still get good results? ....cue the crickets.

It took two years to realize I was looking for secrets no one had to tell. My path forward was obvious. If no one can answer your questions, it's time to come up with your own answers. Strangely, looking inward for answers did not occur to me until I had exhausted every outward possibility. I suspect anything new and useful in any given field comes about in this way. My goal was to recover arrowheads with minimal use of time and resources, regardless of season or conditions. I would be hunting by-the-numbers and finding arrowheads on purpose. My crash course in archaeology took two years. I started reading archaeological society publications, site reports, and historical accounts of Indians. I began to step into the shoes of ancient man. I learned how to make arrowheads with traditional tools and techniques. My eyes began to open.

Two years later it started to come together. I developed techniques using information management and modern technology that gave me leverage when planning a hunt. I call them force multipliers because they allow me to find as many artifacts as a small army. Now I find arrowheads on purpose, consistently, regardless of season or conditions. If you follow the techniques in this book, you will locate Indian camps just by looking at maps. When you leave the house, it will be with the full knowledge you are coming home with arrowheads. The techniques and tools in this book have in their DNA all the information I could gather from those who came before. However, this modern school of arrowhead hunting is truly a different animal. Many of the technologies, strategies, and even the mindset used in this modern school did not exist even a few years ago.

The hobby you pick is your joy, it represents relief from the everyday pressures of life. The feeling you get from any particular hobby is powerful, but can fade over time. Compared to most hobbies, artifact hunting has real staying power. I have met old men in the twilight of their lives, who tell me they feel brand new every time they find an artifact, and some of them have been hunting for 50 years.

William Bauer,

Expert Arrowhead Hunter

Happy Hunting, Willy B.

Chapter 1: Who is an Expert Arrowhead Hunter?

Finding my first arrowhead was an enthralling experience. That first point had such a powerful effect on me, I knew right there and then my life would never be the same. Questions poured out of me like water from a fountain. Where are the arrowheads? How could I find more of them? How many arrowheads were left? Would I have to drive to Texas every time I wanted to find artifacts? Who would answer my questions? I needed an expert.

_____

My First Arrowhead-A look back in time......

A friend of mine videotapes drag races all over the country and makes DVD's. Occasionally I work with him and we go on 12 day over-the-road trips. Drag races are on weekends and this means we have 3 or 4 dead days between events. It's not worth driving 1,000 miles home just to turn around and drive back. Instead of sitting in a hotel room, we go on mini vacations during these days. Usually we attempt to surf the ocean, kayak a river, or hike a national monument.

On this particular trip, my buddy had his heart set on digging arrowheads at a pay dig resort in Texas. To me this was not such a great idea, because I was not even interested in arrowheads. It was $50 per night for cabin rental, and $40 per day for digging fees. Paying $40 for digging in a pit all day didn't sound like a vacation to me. I felt like Tom Sawyer was tricking me into whitewashing the fence. My friend wanted to dig so badly he offered to pay for the whole thing. I reluctantly agreed to go, not expecting to have much fun.

We arrived at Camp Live Oak near Leakey, Texas after a loud weekend of filming drag races. The owner Butch promptly showed us our cabin. The cabin was nice and was made from local stone. The interior walls had geodes and stalagmites embedded in them.

After settling in we returned to the office where Butch was waiting to give us a tour of the digging pits. Turns out most of the grounds encompass an Indian camp on the banks of the Frio River. There were open pits in the field behind the cabin that were 3 or 4 feet deep. We were instructed to dig into the walls of these pits and look through the dirt for artifacts. Butch was even so nice as to loan us a type guide so we could identify our finds. By now it was dark so we went back to our cabin, barbecued some dinner, and contemplated the possibilities of the next day while thumbing through the artifact guide book.

After bacon and eggs we were at it bright and early. Flakes of flint, charcoal from ancient fires, and funny looking rocks were all I was finding for the first two hours. Halfway through my third hour of digging, there it was. The base of an arrowhead was sticking out of the wall. I called my buddy over, and he watched while I wiggled it free.

It was a BEAUTIFUL arrowhead made from tan flint. I stood there, point in my palm, and the world spun around me. I was amazed at its sharpness and the skill that went into its manufacture. I started thinking about the Indian who made it and what he might have looked like. In my hand was an immediate connection to the past. The noise coins make *when they hit the metal tray of a slot machine and all the bells and sirens go off was playing in my head, and the feeling was FANTASTIC!*

I was hooked right then and there, and wanted to find more. I put down my arrowhead and continued digging. Our finds were mostly brokes after that, but one more whole point each before nightfall. We went to the cabin to evaluate our rocks. My first point was a G8 Bulverde, and was between 1,000 and 5,000 years old according to the guide book.

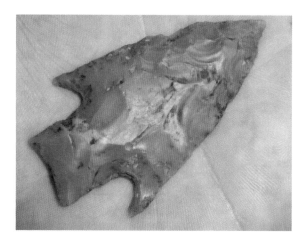

My first arrowhead.

Years passed before I realized how nice that Bulverde really was, or that I had begun hunting arrowheads in a place others only dream of. Not many Bulverde points have their full barbs intact, and the material was Edwards Plateau flint. It was a classic Texas dart point in a classic Texas rock type. In the years since I have returned to where my obsession began. Butch is still there, welcoming as ever. Eventually I became an expert at surface hunting, digging, and even flint knapping. One year I made a 10 inch arrowhead and gave it to Butch, just out of gratitude.

Butch is still in business, you can look him up on the internet. Go visit him if you ever get to Texas, and tell him the Missouri Boys sent you. The funny thing is I still get that same feeling every time I find a nice arrowhead, and it hasn't faded one tiny bit.

Willy B.

My early questions went unanswered. Learning the answers was not just a matter of asking the right person. I spent the first two years following around long-time artifact hunters; they tend to use one method in a handful of spots. They know what works for them, and stick to what works. Long-time artifact hunters are knowledgeable within their experience, but spend a lot of time waiting around for good hunting opportunities.

This would not do for my purposes. I intended to find arrowheads every weekend year round, and anyone who was waiting for rain or spring plowing did not possess knowledge that would help me. With 2 years already invested, it was time to quit asking questions and go find my own answers.

With this frame of mind I decided to apply scientific method to artifact hunting. Scientific method is a body of techniques used for solving problems. Asking the right questions is the key to scientific method. Studying relevant information leads me to develop a theory. Then I test that theory and make conclusions. Applying scientific method is like setting up a line of dominoes. Each proven theory leads to the next good question.

My first question was "what makes someone an expert artifact hunter?"

Right away I realized a huge collection of personal finds does not make someone an expert. Turns out it's not about finding a bunch of arrowheads in a particular location. It's about finding the locations in the first place. Arrowheads are concentrated in Indian camps. By finding the camps, I would find artifacts.

Years later I learned the exact number of Indian camps required to find artifacts every time I left the house. An expert artifact hunter is most easily defined as a person who knows the locations of 50 personally found Indian campsites. This is not an arbitrary number. Only when my site list surpassed 50 was I able to find arrowheads consistently, regardless of season or conditions. Compiling these campsite locations takes time.

Between paying the light bill and raising a family most people will never reach the level of expert artifact hunter, simply because they do not have the time to develop the initial knowledge base. Without this knowledge base you will fail more than you succeed. Few people have the wherewithal to get past these first years, much less breach the 50 campsite barrier. Those who do breathe rarified air.

Within this book lies the salvation of every aspiring expert. I have developed a modern school of artifact hunting and condensed this knowledge in these pages. The theory and technique found here will allow you to bypass these most difficult first years, and operate with the knowledge base of an expert arrowhead hunter, within the time it takes you to read and understand this work.

I make no assumptions of your knowledge base, and have included the basics as well as advanced technique and theory. Each chapter helps explain the next. This book presents a SYSTEM for artifact hunting that involves many disciplines. While there will be individual parts of this book you can apply immediately to improve your artifact hunting results, only by reading this work all the way through will you understand the SYSTEM presented here. This book will give you the tools, but the leg-work is still up to you.

Chapter 2: Why You Will Want A Boat

The Magic Carpet Ride

Floating is a stand-alone hobby. It's the closest you will ever get to a real magic carpet ride. Most people on the river are floating just for the JOY OF FLOATING! Arrowhead hunters are doing it for efficient transportation between Indian campsites, but they enjoy it just the same. You still get the enjoyable experience of floating, even if you don't find any artifacts!

Artifacts are concentrated in Indian camps, and these camps are spaced along creeks, rivers, and lake shores. Your best chance of recovering high quality artifacts is on these campsites. Travel faster between these camps and you will spend more time finding arrowheads and less time just getting around.

All of my mentors hunted on foot. Sure they occasionally canoed a river and hunted it for artifacts, maybe once every couple of years. However they were not PRIMARILY hunting from a boat. Because they were mostly just hiking around, they were prevented from discovering new sites based on the fact that a man walking covers less distance than a man floating. My mentor and some other long-time hunters purchased kayaks AFTER they realized what I was doing, and how effective it was.

Artifact hunting is a numbers game. More hunting opportunities equals more artifacts recovered. In the old days you could just walk around and pick up lots of artifacts. In the modern world you need an advantage if you want old-time results. It's not just a matter of covering miles, but also your physical condition at the end of the day. Hiking in water and climbing up cut-banks all day will really wear you out. Unless it's warm and you can swim across, walking limits you to one side of the bank on big rivers.

A man walking the river covers 3 miles in a day, and then has to walk back to his car. A kayaking man covers 6 miles in a day with ease and then drives home in his waiting car. A man in a motorized boat can cover 12 miles, and then turn around and ride back!

You can start with a relatively inexpensive kayak or canoe, and then work your way up to a john boat with a small outboard for exploring large rivers and lakes. At the high end jet kayaks and duck boats with mud motors will get you farther faster in VERY SHALLOW water, and wave runners are ideal on large lakes.

But don't think for a minute fancy gear ALONE will get you arrowheads. A guy with a $300 kayak and good timing will clean the clock of a guy in a $7000 wave runner with no timing.

Buying a Kayak
I do not recommend buying a canoe. If you have a canoe, use it. Kayaks are a much better investment if you are buying new. Kayaks are easier move, launch, and paddle than canoes. A kayak will draw less water than a canoe, and you

will float through many sections where you would be dragging a canoe. Double ended kayak paddles are literally twice as easy to use as canoe paddles, but you can only use them on kayaks. You sit higher above the water in a canoe and this makes use of a double ended paddle difficult and impractical when canoeing.

Tracking vs. Maneuverability

Tracking is the most important consideration when buying a kayak. Tracking is the ability of a boat to hold a straight line while paddling. If your kayak is too short it will wobble back and forth with each paddle stroke, making forward progress very difficult. The longer the kayak the better it will track in a straight line. There is a trade-off for boat length; loss of ability to maneuver. Longer kayaks are less maneuverable. Maneuverability is very important in fast moving water and can mean the difference between capsizing and staying afloat. You need to be able to avoid obstacles in the river, sometimes on short notice. Both my kayaks are about 10 feet in length, which is the minimum length that gives any tracking at all. I like the 10 foot length because it allows me to whip around river obstacles with great responsiveness.

Weight is a consideration as you will be lifting your kayak when loading and unloading. My Kayak weighs 38 pounds empty. If you buy a long, heavy kayak you will be limited in the places you can launch from.

Two types of kayaks are available, sit on top and sit-inside. A sit on top kayak is basically a giant surfboard with a seat. Sit on tops are GREAT in the summer, but offer no protection from wind or cold weather, and have very little storage. You can use a sit-inside model year round. Both of my kayaks are sit-inside models, although I leave my legs outside on the deck while floating. It's a lot easier to get up and down from the boat with your legs on top of the deck.

If it rains, or if it's cold, I put my legs inside and that offers some protection. A sit-inside kayak allows you to use a kayak skirt, which seals off the opening between you and the cockpit. This is great for rapids or rain. A spray skirt keeps you dry in all seasons.

I travel with my feet on top of the deck most of the time. Nice view, eh?

Having 2 kayaks will allow you to take another person along, which is helpful. Floating alone is dangerous. A second person can drive a second vehicle, which is necessary for the shuttle. The shuttle is how you get back to your car when you have finished your downstream floating route.

Reading the Water

Artifact hunting is best accomplished when water levels are low. Floating at times of low water requires that you look ahead of your boat for underwater obstacles in order to avoid them. Getting up and down from a kayak is not easy and will wear you out if you do it too much. This gets to be a real concern when floating shallow water. You will already be getting in and out at every Indian camp, and sometimes at every gravel bar. When you travel in-between hunting spots your goal is to stay in the kayak and keep floating. If you misread the water, underwater obstacles will stop your forward progress and you will have to stand up and drag your boat to deeper water. Standing up a lot gets VERY tedious and tiring.

Underwater obstacles can easily be avoided by steering around them, but this requires vigilance. The problem is you will be paddling along enjoying yourself and looking at the beautiful scenery and animal life instead of underwater obstacles. When you are in shallow water or rapids you have to maintain vigilance so you can pick a route through river obstacles.

Most mid-sized rivers and small streams are RIFFLE-POOL type waterways. This means shallow riffles and rapids are between deep pools in sequence. You paddle through calm deep pools and float down shallow riffles and rapids. The pools allow you time to chill out and enjoy the scenery or talk to other people. When you reach rapids PAY ATTENTION to the water surface and plan a route ahead of time. Many times I will sit at the edge of a pool above rapids and spend a minute planning a route through fast water and around obstacles.

Things happen QUICKLY in fast moving water, you won't always have time to make adjustments. Planning your route through rapids allows you to successfully navigate them without capsizing (very important in winter!). Plan your route for the ENTIRE stretch of fast moving rapids. If you can't see the end of the rapids around a corner, pull over. Get out and walk down a ways so you can see what you are getting into. If you value your life NEVER float around blind corners in fast moving water. Some stretches of rapids are pretty long, which is fun, but requires MEMORIZATION of your pre-planned route. For example, I might tell myself "stay right in the beginning until you get past the huge boulder, then paddle hard left and out."

Keeping a watch through shallow slower-moving riffles allows you to REMAIN IN YOUR KAYAK instead of having to get up all the time (important YEAR ROUND). Navigating shallow riffles does not require as much pre-planning as rapids, but does require constant vigilance by looking 15 or 20 feet ahead.

The Self Shuttle
When exploring sections of river in a kayak, you want to travel downstream only. This means you need a car waiting at the end of your float, and that usually requires a second vehicle to "shuttle" your car to the take-out(end point) and get you back to the put-in (starting point). If you are floating

alone you need to self-shuttle. I didn't invent the self-shuttle, but I may have perfected it.

The self-shuttle requires planning. I have a cheap mountain bike that I bought at a yard sale for $20. I put new tires on it and did some basic maintenance. It's ugly but reliable and no one wants to steal it. I drive to the launch point and hide my kayak in the woods. I make sure nobody is watching, and cover it with leafy branches if necessary.

Then I drive to the end point of my float and park my vehicle. Now I ride my "throw down" bicycle back to where my boat is hidden, leave the bike in the woods and launch my boat. After floating all day, I arrive at the end where my vehicle is waiting. I load up my boat and drive back to retrieve my bicycle from the starting point. This is a lot of work, but it's the ONLY way you can float by yourself in remote areas. It's really not that big of a deal to ride 5 or 6 miles on a mountain bike. You should FRONT END LOAD a self-shuttle by bicycling FIRST. You are tired out by the end of the day, and you don't want to face a 5 or 6 mile mountain bike ride in the dark.

Kayak Safety
There are trolls in the river. They live under the water. Trolls are always there, waiting to grab your kayak, capsize it, and get a hold of you. The trolls want to pull you under and keep you there, so you stay with them forever in the cold, cold water.

River trolls really do exist, but they aren't creatures of the deep. Trolls are small whirlpools created by eddy currents, and these have the effect of pulling your kayak slightly downward in the water. It feels like you are being GRABBED by something underneath you. River trolls can cause you to capsize. Once you fall out of the boat, you better be wearing a personal flotation device. If you have no life preserver the river trolls REALLY WILL pull you down under the cold, cold water; and they will keep your soul forever.

Wear a full size life preserver and never take it off. I keep my lifejacket on all day regardless of season or temperature. If you are not wearing your life preserver, it can't save your life. The river will kill you as soon as you get comfortable.

Learn some basics before jumping in the river. Go to a local lake and paddle around. You need to know what it feels like to capsize the kayak, and how you will react when trapped upside down, underwater, inside your boat.

You need another person to help you learn this. In 4 feet of water, sit inside your kayak. Have your helper stand next to you and turn you upside down. At first you will panic. You need to remember to push yourself DOWN in order to get out of an overturned kayak. If you don't get out quickly, your helper can turn you upright and keep you from drowning. Practice until you can escape without problems. The secret is to remain calm while underwater and remember to push yourself down and out with your hands on the cockpit edges.

Is learning to kayak worth it? This grouping represents a single day's float in July of 2010. Notice the G10 archaic corner notch, it's thin and has a needle tip. Floating is DEFINITELY worth it!

Float Planning Considerations

Elevation drop is the height water drops over a given distance, expressed in feet per mile. This number determines the speed of the current. You should buy a book of maps made specifically for floating the rivers of your area. The elevation drop will be listed in these books. Float planning information is also available free online.

Less than 2 feet of elevation drop in a mile might as well be one big lake. You need some current to move downstream, without some current you will constantly paddle. Rivers with elevation drops between 2 and 3 feet per mile are tolerable. Any elevation drop between 3 and 10 feet is super fun, but at 10 feet per mile and above, there will be sections of rapids that are dangerous. These sections of rapids are YOU NEED A HELMET territory! If you know what you are doing, 10 feet of elevation drop per mile is exhilarating. You are literally taking your life in your hands running rivers this fast; there is no room for error. Wearing a crash helmet is a REQUIREMENT in fast moving water. It is possible to get out of the river and pull your boat AROUND particularly dangerous sections of rapids.

If you are hunting artifacts limit yourself to 6 miles a day. You need time to hunt the river thoroughly. Check the weather before you leave. Sustained winds of 15 mph will impede your progress and makes hunting difficult. A small rainstorm is ok, but thunderstorms are very dangerous. If a thunderstorm surprises you on the river, get to shore immediately and wait for the lightning to stop before getting back in the water.

Strainers and Logjams

Trees of every size fall into the river on a continuous basis. Any tree in the river creates a hazard that can kill you. These partially sunken trees are referred to as "strainers." If you run into a strainer with your canoe or kayak, your boat will capsize, and you can be trapped in the branches. Many people drown when swift currents hold them underwater against these branches.

It is VERY IMPORTANT to spot these strainers ahead of you, and adjust your course properly. If you can't see around bends in the river, get out of your boat and walk to where you can see to check for strainers. DO NOT run your kayak around fast moving blind turns without looking first. You could easily drown if you hit a strainer in fast moving water.

Many times you can steer around strainers or even float UNDER them! Some of these fallen trees are 80 feet tall and bridge the river bank to bank. In the case of a channel-wide bridge, you might have to pull your boat out of the water and portage around these blockages.

Logjams are deadly. If you have a lightweight kayak, it is possible to CLIMB OVER a logjam and drag your boat over the top. You have to be crazy to walk on a logjam though. If you step on the wrong log, it will sink underneath you. Once you are in the water, the logs come back together, trapping you underneath. Your best course of action is to get out of the water and portage your boat around logjams.

I was floating a 7 mile stretch of river near San Antonio, Texas in August of 2009. Access was difficult and the banks were very steep. There were five logjams in the 7 mile float! There was no way out of the river, the banks were too high. I had no choice but to climb OVER all five logjams. One of the logjams was 20 feet high! The worst part of this float was the water moccasins. These snakes are the most aggressive in North America. They defend their territory against all comers. Water moccasins will try to get INTO your boat, and they will bite you over and over, until they are out of venom. I was chased down twice by moccasins on this float. It was only luck that I was able to paddle away both times. Water moccasins are poisonous and have a flesh eating enzyme in their venom! Anyone who tells you snakes won't bother you if you don't bother them is full of crap. Keep an eye out for marauding water moccasins, and don't mess with Texas.

Night Floating

Floating at night is dangerous and I do not recommend it. However, there are times when night floating gives an artifact hunter the upper hand. This is especially true below hydroelectric dams. Lots of people hunt the river below these dams. Electricity is generated weekdays in the summer during peak demand. The floodgates are opened from middle morning to late afternoon. By dark the water is all the way down. Most people wait until the weekend when no power is produced, and then hunt the banks and gravel bars in daylight while the water is low. If you are brave enough to night float, you can find arrowheads during the week at night, in between power production! Wet arrowheads are easy to spot on a riverbank at night. The flint shines when you hit it with your light. This can be very lucrative.

DO NOT attempt to float at night unless you consider yourself an EXPERT level kayaker. You need to know the section of river you are floating like the back of your hand. If you hit a strainer at night, you are a dead man. To avoid strainers at night, you need to have RECENTLY floated this same section of river in daylight, so you will know the location of strainers ahead of time.

Get a decent LED headlamp, at least 120 lumens of light output. Bring 2 extra sets of batteries just in case. I carry a hand held rechargeable LED spotlight that is waterproof and floats. My spotlight has a 500 lumen output for using at a distance.

Be aware of fog. When you drive in fog your headlights don't penetrate far, and that same thing happens in the river. Your lights will be useless in the fog. You are better off paddling WITHOUT a light on foggy nights, and if you find yourself in this situation you won't enjoy it very much! Stick to the middle of the river, and paddle slowly by the moonlight that filters through. Fog will be produced in massive quantity any time water temperatures are warmer than air temperatures. This means DON'T NIGHT FLOAT IN WINTER! An artifact hunter drowned while night floating in winter in 2010, and he was very experienced.

Spillway hunting IN THE DAYTIME is the second most dangerous type of arrowhead hunting behind scuba diving, but if you spillway hunt by floating at night, you raise the stakes by an order of magnitude. Don't try this unless you REALLY know what you are doing; you probably won't make it back home!

John Boats

John boats are small open aluminum boats 10 to 16 feet in length. John boats are very inexpensive to buy used and can greatly increase your ability to find arrowheads. It is possible to buy a boat/motor/trailer combination for under $1,000.00 but expect to get the motor repaired at some point. If you buy a used motor factor in the cost of getting the motor rebuilt or at least checked out.

Unless you have a full sized pickup truck, you will need to pull a trailer for the john boat. Pulling a trailer is complicated and adds a level of difficulty to any trip. Be sure to carry a spare tire for your trailer and grease the bearings regularly.

I recommend a 14 foot aluminum boat with a 9 hp motor or better. Your boat should be 4 feet wide for good stability. You can buy a jet outboard, but there are many disadvantages to them. They are very expensive and you will have to buy a motor 30% larger due to inefficiencies in outboard jet design. John boats are cheap and plentiful, but be aware they are dangerous in certain circumstances.

John Boat Warnings

John boats are particularly dangerous on big lakes during high winds or thunderstorms. Schedule your hunt for another day if sustained winds are 15mph or higher. You are basically riding an aluminum lightning rod in open water during thunderstorms, and you will be the highest thing around for a thousand feet in any direction. If you want to get THE FEAR, go john-boating on a large lake during a thunderstorm. There are no atheists in a fox hole, and there are no atheists in a john boat during a thunderstorm, either.

Kayaks have supplementary flotation built into them. Foam is injected into bow and stern compartments, and they will not sink, even if completely filled with water. Even the most inexpensive kayak has built-in flotation.

Most john boats DO NOT HAVE supplementary flotation. Once wave heights get taller than the sides of your john boat you are in real danger. If a john boat gets overtopped by waves it will fill up in the blink of an eye, and sink immediately. If you aren't wearing your life preserver you will drown. Whenever you hear on the news "two men drowned today out on the lake" they were probably in a john boat during a surprise storm with no life jackets on.

It's VERY easy to ruin your propeller in rivers due to shallow water obstacles. Propellers are designed with a "shear pin" that can save your prop from being ruined. If you hit a log with your propeller, the shear pin breaks instead of the prop. Be sure to buy some extra shear pins for your propeller so you can replace them when you hit a rock or log. You risk being stranded without extra shear pins.

Motorized Jet Kayaks -WOW!
I started to see REALLY good results in my fourth year of artifact hunting. During that year I logged 372 miles floating. There were many days when I did a self-shuttle or paddled upstream to get to my sites. I was in excellent shape for being 40 years old, but tired of paddling all the time.

MOKAI in the morning fog.
30

Thus began my quest for a motorized boat that would get me to campsites during times of low water. I needed a skinny water boat. Skinny water is a term for shallow water less than 12 inches deep. I began saving money and searched the internet high and low for the BEST possible setup money could buy.

It didn't take long to find the MOKAI motorized jet kayak. These factory direct boats are sold online and are manufactured in the good old USA. They are made in New York, and after reading every review I could get my hands on, I made my decision.

The MOKAI (motorized and kayak put together) is 12 feet long and 3 feet wide with an inboard 7 hp Subaru gasoline engine. The motor was originally designed to power an agricultural water pump. This power plant is paired with an inboard impeller drive unit designed by a rocket scientist (no, really!). It gets 13 miles to the gallon (3 gallon tank) and will carry a 200 pound man at 15 mph. It requires a 12 inch water depth to start, but needs only 4 inches of water to travel full speed once on plane. Water is sucked in through an aluminum grate on the bottom, and thrust out through a 3 inch nozzle in the back.

This costs $5,000.00, but it's the best, and that's what I wanted. It took me a while to save that much, being a broke hillbilly. I ordered it in June of 2011 and it arrived on my lawn by semi-truck in July.

Owning this boat means I never have to self-shuttle, and gives me access to places I only dreamed of before. I always put-in downstream from my goal, that way if I have any mechanical problems I can just float with the current back to my vehicle (once I had a broken throttle cable). No trailer is required for the MOKAI. The inboard engine, impeller drive unit, and gas tank can be removed with quick releases in less than one minute for all three. The hull weighs 100 pounds empty and can be put on top of a car by one man. Weight with motor and full gas tank is 154 pounds.

This is the perfect boat for running shallow rivers. The MOKAI has built in flotation and won't sink even if filled with water, making it safe on large lakes. I recommend the yellow color so others will see you. They make a green model for hunting, but you want other boats to see you at a distance on big rivers and lakes. All fittings on this boat are marine grade stainless steel. It really is an awesome invention.

---

6 Month MOKAI Review

January 2011

I searched the internet for the perfect shallow water vehicle. After looking at every type of drive available, I zeroed in on the MOKAI, a jet powered kayak, as my best available option. I ordered it June 15th 2011, and it was delivered to my yard on July 13th. Twenty five to thirty of these boats are manufactured each month.

The truck driver watched as I opened up the huge box. My yellow MOKAI impressed me immediately with its quality, size, and new boat smell. The truck driver was astounded at the contents of the box. Then a scene unfolded that would repeat itself countless times in the future. "What is that thing? Where did you get it? How much does it cost?"

I was able to remove the engine (to fill oil) with the quick releases without even referring to the manual; the internet videos are great. I registered the boat on the way to the lake and 1 hour later was on the shakedown cruise!

Now 6 months have passed and I have about 400 miles on my MOKAI. The MOKAI really is at its best in a shallow river. Outside of the river environment you would be better off with a regular boat and outboard motor.

15 mph is about the top speed for a MOKAI with an adult and gear (lunch-cooler-ice-etc.). The MOKAI is not a jet ski. If you ride a wave runner and buy one of these-you will not be happy with its speed. If you are a kayaker buying a MOKAI you will be very pleased. 15 mph is about as fast as you can safely navigate a shallow river full of logs and rocks.

You do have to be at full speed and on plane to run in 4 inches of water. 15 mph feels exhilarating as the water gets shallower. If you run the MOKAI up on a gravel bar at full speed (I did that-but not on purpose) gravel will be sucked up the intake. Then you have to get out of the boat to clean the intake grate-no problem when it's warm-but in cold weather you would not be happy getting that wet. The solution is simple-if you are running up onto gravel just let go of the accelerator and kill the motor.

This technique has been successful for me but I REALLY have to pay attention when approaching shallows. This keeps the intake from getting clogged.

Steering is not precise, but it's just good enough allow me to get EXACTLY where I want in this boat. The pull start is very reliable, and the handle is located in front of you in the cockpit, allowing you to start from inside the boat. You have to slowly pull out the starting rope while holding the throttle open, then slowly let the cord back in. Now pull that sucker (the metal foot bar in the floor of the MOKAI allows you to really get a good pull).

It starts on the first pull about 99 % of the time!

The other 1 % of the time it takes 2 pulls. The MOKAI cockpit is very roomy, but don't fill the bow with weight-it makes you plow through the water and you lose speed. A small soft sided cooler fits perfect right next to the seat. If you want to carry a lot of gear-say for overnight camping or diving, tow a dead-man kayak.

I was able to load two 80 cu. ft. scuba tanks, a 30 lb. weight belt and full scuba suit in a 10 foot long old town OTTER kayak. I strapped the tanks to the folded down seat, and covered the cockpit with its travel cover. You can tow that weight a LOT EASEIR than loading down your MOKAI. My speed is reduced to about 10 mph while towing a dead-man kayak, but if you load all that gear into your MOKAI you will go about 5 mph tops.

You can tow your buddies just about ANYWHERE in a MOKAI.

As far as loading goes, even empty the MOKAI is a handful. If you are older, get the trailer, and for sure get the MOKART (a two wheeled cart) no matter what your age. You will need it if you plan on moving the boat in your yard or to your shed like I do. It's not fun to load the MOKAI up on my van roof-but it's do-able for one strong, young person.

In 5 years of hunting this river, I have never seen another motor boat at this spot.

In choppy open water the MOKAI will splash water directly in your face most of the time it's moving forward into waves; not big rollers but small chop. It handles big rolling waves just fine, even sideways.

A spray skirt will not alleviate this- but a windshield works great. A snowmobile windshield will fit if you modify it. This water in the face thing will REALLY get you down on a big open lake with waves--you either need a windshield or a mask and snorkel-it's your choice.

Gas mileage is awesome-went 23 miles on my longest single day trip, and still had a gallon left at the end of the day.

The footprint of this boat is the smallest you can get and still feel safe on a big lake. It's very stable, and has a ton of flotation. I can easily mount the MOKAI in deep water by climbing up the nose. I would not want to go out on a lake in the green MOKAI, but the yellow is highly visible.

This special purpose skinny water boat will get you safely up river, around and over logs, under low hanging river canopy and into spots where you can't go on foot-and you can bring 30 lbs. of gear without affecting performance (I weigh 170lbs). If you want a water toy buy a jet ski. This machine is not made for that. This boat is made for the special purpose of getting where others cannot go, and doing it RELIABLY and SAFELY.

I am VERY PLEASED with the quality, reliability, and well thought out features of this boat. The MOKAI is at its best in a shallow river. If you are in lakes mostly, you would be better off with a john boat and an outboard.

The best features of this boat are -
1. It does not require a trailer. Load it on a roof rack!
2. It goes UPSTREAM in only 4 inches of water.

3. Only one car required for river trips-put in and go upstream as far as you want, then turn off the motor and FLOAT QUIETLY BACK! Sometimes I drop my buddies off upstream and then put the MOKAI in at the takeout and run upstream towards them-still just one car needed.

4. It goes over submerged logs and under river canopy-where even kayaks can't go.

5. Awesome gas mileage-40 miles for 3 gallons!

6. Super reliable starting and running.

7. Noise is not an issue. Sounds like my push lawnmower. One kayaker heard me from a distance and later told me it sounded like someone was mowing the river. I have the Subaru motor-older models have a Honda that is louder.

The negative points of this boat are -

1. Not very good for open water/lakes-especially with oncoming waves/wind.

2. Not useable during fall when leaves come down from trees. Leaves clog intake grate every 1/2 mile. First three weeks of November MOKAI is not useable in rivers or streams.

3. Intake grate is difficult to clean. Gravel gets jammed in grate and requires a screwdriver to get it out. This means getting your entire arm wet for several minutes-not fun in winter. Try to avoid running up onto gravel bars at speed. This is more difficult than it sounds!

4. Moss clogs intake grates even at idle. AVOID mossy bedrock in shallow water.

Conclusion: Single vehicle river runs and shallow water running are the reasons to buy this boat.   In the river, NOTHING BEATS A MOKAI. In the river, the MOKAI outperforms ANY outboard motor boat, canoe, kayak, or even an airboat. Air boats cannot pass under logs blocking the river. There have been several instances where I have come upon people dragging their canoes in the river where it was too shallow for them to paddle. I was able to pass by them at 15 mph.

I was on a large federally navigable river when I came around the bend to find 4 bass boats stopped. The hydroelectric dam was shut off miles upstream, and the water was down to only 3 feet. None of the bass boats could navigate up the newly exposed rapids to the next pool. I passed right by them and went up the rapids like it was a golf green and I was riding a kart. It was a smooth and deliberate glide right up the length of the chute! Driving the MOKAI up rapids is VALUABLE, but the looks on people's faces when they watch you do this are PRICELESS!

This summer's drought kept me out of small streams. Falling lake levels exposed entire forests on local lake bottoms. Once fully submerged, these forests now have only 2 feet of water. ONLY the MOKAI was able to navigate the sunken forest. The MOKAI is the ultimate skinny-water craft. Boldly goes where no other motor boats even try. LOVE my MOKAI.

Happy Boating,
Willy B.

Duck Boats and Mud Motors

Duck boats with mud motors are made for duck hunting, and are an excellent way to navigate shallow muddy swamps and marshes. These units use a prop and they are AWESOME but really expensive. It costs about $15,000.00 for a full sized boat 16' hull/motor/trailer combination. Mud motors have skegs that keep the propeller from hitting the bottom, rocks, or logs. On long-tail models the propeller shaft can be 8 feet or more in the horizontal plane. You can actually travel OVER small gravel bars at full speed with a long-tail mud motor/duck boat combo. You can buy a smaller version for about $5,000.00 (boat/motor/trailer). You need at least a 12 hp long-tail mud motor to power a small 12 foot aluminum duck boat with 2 people in it.

I am saving up for one of these units so I can go into muddy marshes. The MOKAI's jet doesn't like swamp grass, and the mud motor can run through JUST MUD with no water. These mud motors are great for what they were designed to do, but NOTHING beats a MOKAI in a shallow river. The MOKAI can travel UP long sections of shallow rocky rapids in only 4 inches of water without damaging the drive unit. No other boat can do that.

Chapter 3: Finding vs. Buying
Arrowheads as a Commodity

Arrowhead hunters are collecting what money cannot buy. Artifact hunters collect experiences, memories of adventure, excitement, and triumph beyond the capacity of most people. They see things and do things that others only dream of.

When you go to the movies, you pay your money and you are allowed to live vicariously through others for a couple of hours. You aren't actually doing anything but paying your money. We all enjoy movies and they don't require any personal risk. Movies provide the guaranteed result of entertainment. Buying an arrowhead is like going to the movies.

When you find your own arrowheads you are no longer watching a movie, you are IN the movie.

Because artifact hunting is so difficult, the vast majority of artifact collectors buy points to fill the gaps in their frames. There are pure hunters and pure buyers, and plenty of overlap in between, but everyone wants to find their own arrowheads. Everyone wants to be the hero of their own story.

Hunters who collect only their own finds are purists. These purists maintain a level of authenticity in their collections that bought collections can never achieve. Authentic arrowheads are valuable, but authentic adventures are priceless. Every point in my frame represents an adventure where I overcame long odds, many times at great personal risk. This type of accomplishment cannot be bought or sold. Arrowhead hunting is not about owning pointy rocks. Owning pointy rocks is arrowhead collecting, and that's an entirely different subject.

The Arrowhead Mall

First a person finds an arrowhead inadvertently while doing activities unrelated to arrowhead hunting. Immediately they are fascinated and want to find more. They search the internet for arrowhead hunting advice, and then go try to find artifacts. A new hunter generally has limited success, and realizes it will take many years to build a decent collection.

Then this new person goes to an artifact show. He sees case after case of the most fantastic looking, incredibly colorful, perfect artifacts. It takes about 5 minutes to understand that most of this stuff is for sale. Welcome to the arrowhead mall, where dreams can be bought.

Heck, it would be a LOT easier to just buy some points and frame them on my wall. Probably would be cheaper in the long run, too. Add up the cost of gas and the time it takes to find even crude and broken artifacts and that amount of money can buy some nice points. Seems like a pretty good deal buying artifacts, and for sure it's the ONLY way a new hunter is going to put G9 artifacts in his frame on a regular basis.

Not everyone has what it takes to hunt arrowheads. Most people will be collecting through buying. The problem is buying Indian artifacts is like walking across a minefield. It is conservatively estimated that over a million arrowheads are made every year by amateur and commercial flint knappers. These modern-made pieces are often passed off as authentic and sold to collectors who pay hundreds of dollars per piece.

Inexperienced collectors depend on authenticating services that provide COA's (certificates of authenticity). Authenticators have microscopes and black lights, and most of them have handled a lot of authentic points. This seems pretty foolproof to a new collector. People who buy artifacts will tell you there are arrowheads that are "no brainers" and are obviously authentic. While this may be true if you have a decade of experience handling personal found artifacts from your area, it's not true for inexperienced collectors.

Keep in mind arrowheads in the collector market are a commodity, nothing more. You should buy artifacts with one of two strategies. Buy what makes you happy, or buy with the idea of making a profit. If you are buying what pleases you with no intention of selling, you can never be ripped off. If you are buying with profit as your goal, look for COA's from well-known authenticators.

Collectors who buy and sell will argue buying artifacts is no different than collecting antiques, stamps, or civil war relics. Buyers will tell you "sure there are fakes, and you need someone with more experience to tell you these things are authentic and not purpose-made to deceive."

Maybe there is some scientific means of laboratory testing civil war relics, antique furniture, coins, and stamps. But,

THERE IS NO SCIENTIFIC METHOD FOR AGE TESTING ARROWHEADS. Let me repeat that. THERE IS NO SCIENTIFIC METHOD FOR AGE TESTING ARROWHEADS.

COA's are not certifying authenticity. COA's are more accurately certifying an arrowhead is not OBVIOULSY FAKE. That is the most any human with all the best laboratory testing equipment could say.

Collecting arrowheads, antiques, civil war relics, or stamps is all very similar. The difference with arrowheads is that no one is furiously knapping a million fake stamps per year. People are knapping as a hobby, and that means they are doing it on a regular basis for fun. Thousands of people are not making civil war relics on a regular basis for fun. Thousands of people are not making coins on a regular basis for fun. Thousands of people ARE knapping millions of arrowheads on a regular basis for fun. Inevitably some of these modern-made points end up in the authentic market.

Most authenticators are honest and scrupulous, but even the best make mistakes. Most of them have very little incentive to kill (certify as modern) arrowheads that are not obviously fake. They need repeat customers, and these customers are putting food on their table. Unless it's got copper tool marks all over it or some other trait that makes it obviously fake, it's going to get a COA. Keep in mind there are NO STANDARDS for authenticators. Anyone can be an authenticator just by claiming to be one. Certain authenticators have better reputations than others, though. Ask other collectors, they will tell you which authenticators are the most trusted.

Ultimately, does it really matter if the rocks you are buying were made a long time ago? Resale only depends on magic pieces of paper called COA's, not actual authenticity. Resale has nothing to do with an arrowhead being made by an ancient Indian.

There is no question that undetectable fakes exist.

The Disturbing Genius of Woody Blackwell
December 2012

The most talented knapper in the world is a fellow named Woody Blackwell. Woody knaps points with such skill and precision, you would swear he was a vampire. In Woody's younger days he knapped a group of Clovis points using aboriginal tools and techniques. Woody did this so perfectly, archaeologists with doctorate degrees authenticated them. Never mind authenticators, these were highly educated scientists using all the laboratory techniques they could muster. Woody was able to sell a handful of these points for $80,000.00 to some big league collectors. Although no direct scientific method for dating arrowheads exists, there are ways to determine where some types of stone originate.

Fortunately for us, Woody made one mistake. A single Clovis point from the group he sold was made from quartz crystal that came from Brazil. How could a point supposedly recovered in North America be made from a material found only in South America? This would be rare indeed, if it were even possible.

If the quartz woody used had come from Arkansas, no one would have been the wiser, or asked any more questions. None of the other points in the group showed ANY characteristics that would indicate they were not of ancient manufacture, and all of the lithics used to manufacture the rest of the group were sourced from within the continental USA.

But, the jig was up. Woody confessed, and refunded all parties. If Woody hadn't included one Brazilian quartz point in the group, undetectable fakes would have remained unknown, and we would not be able to say with absolute certainty "undetectable fakes exist."

Today Mr. Blackwell is a highly respected commercial knapper who sells his pieces as modern through his website. Most of the points Woody makes now are so large and the material he uses so fantastic they are obvious art pieces. Many admire Woody for his ability to do what they said couldn't be done, reverse engineer authentic paleo points so well that nobody could tell they were reproductions.

Willy B.

Remember, if it looks too good to be true, it is too good to be true. It can still be fun buying and selling, even though there are many pitfalls and genuinely disturbing concerns. Many people find buying and selling artifacts in the collector market a rewarding experience, both personally and financially. Once the artifact leaves the hands of the original finder, it's just a commodity. Like anything else bought and sold, BUYER BEWARE.

Point Grading Systems

For communication to be effective, a common set of terms is required. The purpose of a point grading system is to allow accurate communication between people. Artifacts are graded by collectors on a G1 through G10 basis. G1 being the lowest grade, and G10 the highest grade.

Most arrowheads found are "field grade arrowheads." This means they compare to points found in plowed fields that have been damaged by the plow. Field grade is anything G5 or below. G6 and G7 points are rare. Flaking, size, and symmetry are above average. G8 and G9 points are rare and perfect, but lack a little bit in size, thinness, or symmetry. G10 points are perfect in size, thinness, and symmetry. G10 is an EXTREMELY RARE grade. The average arrowhead hunter who hunts for 25 years will have one G10 point in the center of his frame, maybe five G8's and 2 G9's surrounding it, and 312 lower grade points, mostly G5's.

If you follow the system in this book you will do much better. It all depends on the number of opportunities you have to hunt. Artifact hunting is a numbers game. More hunting opportunities equal more artifact finds. My hunting habits are 2 days a week 52 weeks a year. I spend my vacation in Texas digging arrowheads, and take a handful of multi day float trips to remote areas.

Best Finds 2011. Red spot Langtry G10 (top left), Friday Bi-face G10 (center), orange stained Dickson G10 (top right), and four G9 points an EXCEPTIONAL YEAR! Two of these are riverbank finds, two are dug, two are from lakeshores, and one is a plowed field find. The orange Dickson and the green dart point (bottom right) were found ON THE SAME DAY in camps 20 miles apart!

What Makes a G10 Point?

G10 Drill found in construction dirt in 2010. Whatever it was used for, it definitely never drilled anything.

Flint knapping is accurately PREDICTING how stone will break. There will NEVER be flawless manufacture in flint knapping. CONTROLLED BREAKAGE? Oxymoron if I ever heard one.

However, perfection does exist. G10 artifacts are the ultimate in working skill and control. The knapper of a G10 has produced an artifact of EXCEPTIONAL workmanship, being as thin and perfectly shaped as the technique and materials would allow. The finished product is as near perfect as possible a match to the knappers preconceived idea.

Defining obscenity is very subjective, but you know it when you see it. A G10 artifact is kind of like obscenity. You know a G10 when you see it.

Salted Fields and Fake Finds
"I found it, of course it's real." --old time Charlie.

There are many reasons people might plant a modern made artifact in the field for someone else to find.

_____

Old Time Charlie
June 2012

This is a story told to me in the living room of a well-known authenticator (some of you would recognize his name) and I believe it to be true. I might not have all the details perfect, it's been a few years back. This is not meant to dissuade any of you from hunting, digging, buying, or selling. But you should be aware of it.

A local old time collector/hunter (we will call him old time Charlie) met an arrowhead hunter in the field who was new to

48

the area.   Old time Charlie has FORGOTTEN more about arrowheads than you know.   He has been hunting and collecting for 40 years.

Charlie and new guy ran into each other on the same hunting spot several times, and the new guy told old time Charlie he had permission to dig a local shelter known to Charlie (new guy did have permission) and that if Charlie would agree to share/split any finds they might make-new guy would take old time Charlie with him to dig.

Sounded reasonable to Charlie-so they went digging a few days later.   Old time Charlie finds a 4 1/2 inch calf creek, better than any calf creek he has EVER seen, and it's a religious experience for him.

Charlie sticks with their agreement and decides to sell the find and split the money with new guy.   Charlie calls everyone he knows and tells them about his new find.   Charlie is an old dude, known as rock solid in the collector community.   Charlie shows this rock to the right people, tells them where he dug it, and they promptly write him a check for $18,000.00 without getting any outside opinions, on old time Charlie's word alone.   Charlie cashes the check and happily gives new guy $9,000.00 cash.

The buyer goes to get it authenticated----MASSIVE FAIL, it's an obvious fake.   The point is found to have been BOUGHT ON EBAY from a knapper for $28.00.

Apparently new guy set all this up, and now new guy has left town. Old time Charlie is not a wealthy fellow, and ends up borrowing against his house to pay back the money.

"Of course it's real, I dug it up myself."--old time Charlie.

It could happen to anyone.

Willy B.

Some fields are salted with fakes for reasons that seem good to the person doing the planting. Maybe you want to make sure your young son finds an arrowhead, only he never finds the fake you planted for him.

I know of one case where a man was dying of cancer and his friends arranged for him to find a large Dalton spear point on one of his regular hunting spots. This was the "find of a lifetime" for the guy with cancer, and everything worked out great until the man tried to sell it a few months later and found out it was modern made.

Malicious reasons for planting artifacts include revenge and anger. I know another case where fake arrowheads were planted in large numbers on a gravel bar by a landowner, who was angry at the general public for hunting what he considered "his gravel bar."

Landowners get the short end of the stick sometimes, too. One landowner got tired of being beat to his own plowed field site by some neighbors, so he confronted them and ran them off. The neighbors knew he often posted his finds on the internet, so they planted a couple of nice fake slate artifacts. The landowner found them after the next rain, and promptly posted photos of his finds online. Some experienced collectors noted that the slate artifacts looked fake just from seeing the online photos. The slate finds were fakes, and the finder was embarrassed. It could happen to anyone.

Fortunately few people have the time, resources, or motivation to throw modern made artifacts out into nature. Salting of fields and rivers is not very common, but it does happen, and is something you should be aware of.

Typology

Arrowheads are classified into types by archaeologists and collectors. Types are named by the first guy who dug them in a controlled, scientific context. Some are named for people, some are named for locations, and some are named for their resemblance to other objects. These names are completely arbitrary and are not to be taken too seriously.

The type names of artifacts are useful in the sense that a common set of terms is necessary for good communication between people. If I tell you I found a Clovis point, you know that is a rare paleo-indian artifact 13,000 years old. You would know it was a lanceolate point without notches and that it probably has at least one flute on its base. You would also know it is probably between 1 and 4 inches in length and has a thickness to width ration of about 1:5. It's a lot easier to say "Clovis point" than all the other information the name implies. This makes learning type names useful. There are entire books with hundreds of pages of types and names and the placement of each temporally. Placement of point shapes along a time line based on carbon dates is very useful to artifact hunters and archaeologists alike. Determining your arrowhead type is best accomplished with an Indian artifact type guide.

Avoid arrowhead type guides that contain pricing information. The value of an artifact is determined by what a person will pay you for it on a given day. Your best bet for pricing information is viewing catalogues from completed auctions that contain the price each piece sold for. Arrowheads pictured as examples in type guides written by archaeologists are authentic examples obtained in the field, which is not always the case in pricing guides. Arrowhead type guides that include prices for artifacts will publish pictures of anyone's artifacts in their books for a fee, many times without personally viewing or authenticating the artifact.

Guides that cover all of North America are biting off more than they can chew. Be sure to look for a REGIONAL type guide. Most authenticators specialize in a single area, and a good type guide will do the same. Don't worry too much if you can't find a type in your arrowhead guide that matches the point you found. There are MANY unnamed types that exist in between named types. For example, I have found points with characteristics of two different point types. These are called transitional points. There was no straight line conversion from one point style to another along a timeline. Styles of manufacture in stone tools were passed from father to son through family groups as the skill was taught to young children. The characteristics of any given tool changed over time as individuals figured out new ways to make artifacts that improved the tool's usefulness or made its manufacture easier.

Exotic Lithics

Arrowheads are made from many different types of stone, but not all stone was created equal. An exceptionally lustrous, colorful, or rare material is considered an "exotic lithic." When an artifact is made from one of these exotic types of stone, it bumps the grade up one level.

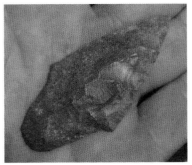

This plowed field find is red oolitic chert Waubesa dart point.

Oolitic material is characterized by small shperes within the material.

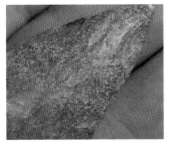

Use of exotic stone is more common in paleo age points. Many of the oldest point types show workmanship and materials far beyond what was necessary to get the job done. My theory is that paleo-indians thought these exotic materials and extra-fine workmanship gave power to their stone points and aided them in having safe and successful hunts. The archeological record shows paleo-indians hunted mega-fauna, large animal species now extinct. Hunting wooly mammoths and giant buffalo was a lot more dangerous than hunting white tail deer.

When these mega-fauna died out, maybe it was no longer necessary for Indians to seek out exotic materials or make projectile points with extra care, as hunting smaller animals was not as risky to their personal safety. If you missed a spear throw at a mammoth, you might be killed. You would probably not risk death if you missed a spear throw at a white tail deer. Once the EXTRA LARGE game died out, it wasn't nearly as dangerous to hunt the smaller game that was left. Archaic and woodland period hunts would not have been as risky as paleo-indian period hunts.

This is one theory as to why Indians might have used exotic materials, styles, and intricate workmanship in their stone tool making. Sometimes when I find a particularly well made point fashioned from an exotic lithic, I wonder if that particular point was saved for a special purpose by the Indian who made it. Did they have an appreciation for extra-beautiful, finely made stone tools like we do? I like to think the answer is YES.

Chapter 4: Arrowheads and the Law

Is Indian Arrowhead Hunting Legal?

This is a simple question with complicated answers. Every state has different laws; some states are very permissive, and others have game wardens waiting to jump out from behind the bushes and ticket you for picking up an arrowhead. It's very important to learn your state laws before attempting to hunt Indian artifacts in public waterways.

Laws All States Have in Common

Disturbing human burials or even digging where burials are suspected is illegal. If you accidentally discover human remains, you are obligated to report the find to local law enforcement. Digging burial mounds is 100% illegal, even on you own private property.

It is illegal to pick up an artifact or dig for artifacts in a state park.

The Archaeological Resources Protection Act of 1979

This piece of work is a federal law that criminalizes arrowhead hunting on ALL federally owned public lands. It is a misdemeanor to pick up an arrowhead on federal land, and a felony to dig artifacts on federal land. Federal land includes National Parks, military installations, Bureau of Land Management properties, Corp of Engineers Reservoirs, National Forests, and all state owned Conservation land managed by the Corp of Engineers. This act also cracks down on trafficking of illegally obtained artifacts. It is a felony to engage in selling, purchasing, or interstate transport of artifacts removed in violation of federal, state, and local regulations.

Well, What Can I Do?

Surface hunting private property is your safest bet in any state. It is LEGAL to surface hunt private property with landowner permission. GET PERMISSION FIRST. You would be guilty of trespass for just walking on someone else's land; pick up an arrowhead and you would be guilty of theft. DO NOT TRESPASS. Getting a ticket or being arrested is the LEAST of your worries. You can get SHOT trespassing, and you won't be alive to give your side of the story.

In some states it is LEGAL to dig on private property, as long as no human burials are disturbed, and no state permits are required. Again, be sure to get landowner permission.

Some states allow surface hunting on public waterways, but many states are heavily regulated, and it's up to you to KNOW YOUR STATE LAWS. State laws are subject to change; you need to contact your state archaeologist or your state archaeological society to learn what is legal in your state. Contact information is given at the end of this chapter for all 50 states and US territories.

Consider the politics of arrowhead hunting BEFORE confronting an archaeologist about state arrowhead hunting laws. Archaeologists will often make negative assumptions about you and your intentions and may not give you accurate information unless you approach them in the correct manner. Tell them you want to know how to ethically and legally hunt artifacts.

Landowner Confrontation: It's Inevitable

Many States allow artifact hunting in federally navigable waterways (most rivers big enough for john boats are federally navigable). However many people who own land along these rivers do not know the law and will attempt to run you off anyway. If you see a landowner approaching you on the river, it's best to move on before they confront you. It's a lot easier in the long run and the situation can deteriorate rapidly. Don't worry about anyone calling the sheriff, its way better to deal with a deputy than some angry armed hillbilly.

If you get confronted, just leave. DO NOT stand around and get verbally abused by a landowner. Standing up for your rights in this situation is more trouble than it's worth. Most of the time during a landowner confrontation, the landowner will start to feel like he has got you "over a barrel" and he will begin to threaten to call the law on you and start demanding that you tell him your name or show him your identification. You do not have to show anyone other than a lawman your identification. Landowners have no authority over citizens on public navigable waterways.

You need to cut the conversation off by saying this "I did not think I was trespassing. You have told me I am. Now I am leaving." Then you turn your back and walk away. Do not turn around or engage the landowner after that NO MATTER

WHAT he says. The longer you try to talk to one of these disgruntled landowners the worse your situation becomes. Move along. The next gravel bar is probably better, anyway!

Missouri State Water Law

It took me a long time to figure out Missouri water law, and EVERY STATE IS DIFFERENT. The following information was obtained by reading Missouri court cases dating back decades. It was difficult to locate this information, and to translate the "legalese." LAWS CHANGE. Ignorance of the law is no excuse, and you will be held accountable for your actions. Contact your state archaeologist or state archaeological society for current information. It is YOUR RESPONSIBILITY to know your current state laws. That having been said, the following information will benefit your overall knowledge of legal terms and definitions applicable to your own state's water law. To be clear, the information below applies ONLY to the state of Missouri, and you need to look up your own state's law.

What is the Legal Relationship between citizens, landowners, water, rocks, and fish?

First, do not even pick up rocks in Corp of Engineer Lakes, parks, or federally managed Conservation land. It's illegal under all circumstances to remove artifacts from federal lands and parks in all 50 states.

HOWEVER there is a legal basis for artifact hunting on what amounts to a public highway (navigable stream) in the state of Missouri.

There is no written list of water laws directly stating what is and isn't legal on Missouri waterways. Our system is riparian restrictive water law. That means existing court cases establish the law that is applied today. By reading to the decisions in previous cases you will know what is legal.

Once you get past the words they use, it's not that complicated. A riparian landowner is someone who owns property next to a waterway or lake. Waterways are classed as federally navigable, state navigable or non-navigable.

Federally Navigable waterways are large rivers which can be or have been historically used for commercial purposes. In the past many rural Missourians made and sold railroad ties for extra income and floated them to market on creeks flooded by spring rains. This has set historical precedent for commercial use of many creeks and rivers in the state.

State Navigable waterways only require that you can "reasonably float it for travel or recreation with a canoe or small craft". The Corp of Engineers keeps track and if you call your local Corp office they will tell you what streams are state or federally navigable.

Non-Navigable waterways are privately owned and you should not even walk there without permission from a landowner. These are streams so small no boat could float them, even a kayak. Spring branches are considered non-navigable.

Federal and state navigable waterways in the state of Missouri have an EASEMENT that supersedes land titles. If you own property along a navigable waterway you are a riparian landowner and subject to this easement, even though your deed says "to the middle of the river bottom."

This means even if you own both sides of a navigable stream you DO NOT OWN the water or anything in it-including fish, rocks, or the bottom-from normal (not flood level) high water mark to high water mark. The bottom of a navigable waterway is considered a public highway.

Riparian landowners (those who own land next to a river, creek or lake) can remove gravel or rocks from the water, and take it to their property, but do not OWN the gravel until they move it out of the public waterway.

It is legal to fish, wade, or swim in a navigable waterway, and to be on a gravel bar from high water line to high water line. Not the "100 year flood" line, but the "obvious high water mark." This is why I prefer hunting below hydroelectric dams. Power producing dams often change water levels in a river by 10 feet or more on a daily basis. This fluctuation leaves OBVIOUS high water marks on the banks, clearly establishing your legal limit for collecting arrowheads.

In other words, in Missouri it is legal for you to be on the river, and even to hunt artifacts. Archaeologists and Corp personnel told me it was legal to surface hunt water line to water line. You are not disturbing sites in context when they are being washed away.

Missouri water law establishes a citizen's rights for floating and recreation, but it won't keep you from getting verbally abused, chased off, or shot. Many landowners think they own the river bottom because it says so on their deed, and you aren't going tell them any different. 99% of landowners have never heard of an "easement" that supersedes their land title. It's easier to just move along. Try to avoid confrontations in the first place.

Remember all the above information applies ONLY to Missouri, your state will be different, and probably not as good from an arrowhead hunters point of view. Eastern states tend to have better water laws than western states.

Your State's Water Law
Call your state archaeologist and ask if surface hunting is legal in your state, regardless of any advice or laws listed here. Laws can change over time, and just because it was legal when I wrote this does not mean it will remain legal. Most archaeologists want all forms of artifact hunting made illegal, and if it isn't already that way in your state, they are trying to get it done RIGHT NOW. Remember that these state archaeologists are NOT YOUR FRIEND and will consider you a criminal without getting to know you first, just based on the fact that you are hunting artifacts without a magic piece of paper (a degree in anthropology). Approach them carefully and be aware of their prejudice against arrowhead hunters.

Listed below are the current names and numbers for the State Archaeologists in every state at the time of this writing. Call your state archaeologist up and ask him if surface hunting is legal in your state. Archaeologists DO NOT LIKE artifact hunters, and paint them with a broad and NEGATIVE brush. Don't call up this guy and tell him you plan to dig up archaeological sites. Reassure him you just want to find out how to hunt legally and ethically in your state. He will probably broach the subject of digging without you bringing it up. Keep your expectations low and just try to get some good information on artifact hunting laws.

He will suggest that you join your local archaeological society. This is a good idea for a beginner. You can meet like-minded people who can help you find hunting spots and learn how to get landowner permission. However, be aware that many archaeological societies are run by local archaeologists and their graduate students. Some of these societies, such as the Missouri Archaeological Society, are actively attempting to make arrowhead hunting illegal, even surface hunting on public waterways. I joined my state society for one year, but once I figured out what they were doing, I stopped giving them money.

Some states have very good policies for surface hunting and even digging Indian artifacts, while in other states camouflaged agents are hiding in the riverbanks waiting to arrest anyone picking up a rock. Arkansas, California, and Florida are the worst I know of. Washington and Oregon are also highly regulated.

It is your responsibility to KNOW YOUR CURRENT STATE LAW before hunting.

I have included information for some states based on my personal experience. I have included the actual state laws for some states, but these are subject to change, and you need to CHECK FOR YOURSELF. Ignorance of the law is not an excuse for breaking it. In many cases, right and wrong have very little to do with laws. But it is what it is, and the law demands respect.

REMEMBER: It is 100% illegal to pick up artifacts on Corp of Engineer Lakes, BLM Lands, National Forest Lands, and both Federal and State Parks in ALL 50 states. Don't do it, you will get arrested, fined, and you can even be jailed. First offense is a $275 fine, for just picking an artifact up off the ground.

State Archaeologist Contact Information

Alabama
Stacye Hathorn,
State Archaeologist
Alabama Historical Commission
468 South Perry Street
Montgomery, AL 36130-0900
Phone: (334) 230-2649
Fax: (334) 262-1083
Email: stacye.hathorn@preserveala.org
Visit the Archaeological Services of the Alabama Historical Commission at www.preserveala.org/

In 2012 Alabama actually had some pro-collector legislation pass the house and senate, but I don't know if it got signed into law by the governor. This state has been notorious for arresting artifact hunters and divers looking for arrowheads or civil war relics on public rivers.

Alaska
J. David McMahan
State Archaeologist/Deputy SHPO
Alaska Department of Natural Resources
Office of History and Archaeology
550 W. 7th Avenue, Suite 1310
Anchorage, AK 99503-5921
Phone: (907) 269-8723
Fax: (907) 269-8908
Email: dave.mcmahan@alaska.gov
Visit the Alaska Department of Natural Resources at
http://www.dnr.state.ak.us/parks/oha/

American Samoa
David J. Herdrich
Territorial Archaeologist/Deputy HPO
Executive Offices of the Governor
American Samoa Historic Preservation Office
American Samoa Government
Pago Pago, AS 96799
Phone: (684) 699-2316
Fax: (684) 699-2276
Email: David_J_Herdrich@samoatelco.com
Visit the American Samoa Historic Preservation Office at
ASHPO.org

Arizona
Todd Pitezel

Assistant Curator, Archaeology
Arizona State Museum
University of Arizona
PO Box 210026
Tucson, AZ 85721-0026
Phone: (520) 621-4795
Email: pitezel@email.arizona.edu
Visit the University of Arizona's Arizona State Museum at
www.statemuseum.arizona.edu and check up on their
Archaeological Research at
www.statemuseum.arizona.edu/arch

Arkansas
Ann M. Early
State Archeologist
Arkansas Archeological Survey
2475 North Hatch Avenue
Fayetteville, AR 72704
Phone: (479) 575-3556
Fax: (479) 575-5453
Email: amearly@uark.edu
Visit the at Arkansas Archaeological Survey at
www.uark.edu/campus-resources/archinfo or
www.arkansasarchaeology.org

This state has a checkered past when it comes to Indian artifact hunting. For many years people were digging Indian graves and taking grave goods including "head pots" and flint artifacts. Skeletons were left spread all over the ground and there was no law against it.

So the Arkansas legislature over-reacted and passed a law that was EXTREME. It reads something like "you cannot break the ground in search of artifacts in the state of Arkansas." It is not legal to even pick up arrowheads on state owned lands or navigable rivers anywhere in the state. If you have permission to surface hunt from an Arkansas landowner you would be ok. It is NOT legal for a landowner to dig his own land for Indian artifacts.

Don't mess around in Arkansas, they have conservation agents and game wardens in SWAT gear hiding in the forest just waiting to arrest arrowhead hunters. These agents are specially trained at week long seminars on arresting artifact hunters. These agents cannot be fooled, and know EXACTLY what to look for in identifying who is a serious arrowhead hunter.

California
Michael D. McGuirt
Associate State Archaeologist
Office of Historic Preservation
P.O. Box 942896
Sacramento, CA 94296-0001
Phone: (916) 653-2716 and (916) 653-8920
Fax: (916) 653-9824
Email: mmcguirt@ohp.parks.ca.gov
Visit the California State Parks' Office of Historic Preservation at http://www.ohp.parks.ca.gov/

California is one of the most over-legislated states in the union. It's illegal to pick up artifacts on public lands or public waterways. This state is anti-collector, and they have LOTS of game wardens looking to arrest ANYONE doing ANYTHING that looks funny. But, you can smoke all the devil-weed you want if you have your California state issued weed-smoking license!-go figure.

Colorado
Richard Wilshusen
State Archaeologist/Deputy SHPO - Archaeology
History Colorado
Office of the State Archaeologist
1200 Broadway
Denver, CO 80203
Phone: (303) 866-2736
Fax: (303) 866-2711
Email: Richard.Wilshusen@state.co.us
Visit History Colorado's Office of Archaeology & Historic Preservation at
http://www.historycolorado.org/archaeologists/office-archaeology-historic-preservation

Connecticut
Nicholas Bellantoni
State Archaeologist
Office of the State Archaeologist
Connecticut State Museum of Natural History & Connecticut Archaeology Center
University of Connecticut
Unit 1023

2019 Hillside Road
Storrs, CT 06269-1023
Phone: (860) 486-5248
Fax: (860) 486-0827
Email: Nicholas.Bellantoni@UConn.edu
Visit the Connecticut Office of State Archaeology at
http://www.cac.uconn.edu

Delaware
Faye Stocum
DE DHCA Archaeology Lab
c/o Zwaanendael Museum
102 Kings Highway
Lewes, DE 19958
Phone: (302) 645-7231
Fax: (302) 645-7297
Email: faye.stocum@state.de.us
Visit the Delaware State Historic Preservation Office at
www.state.de.us/shpo/index.htm

District of Columbia
Ruth Trocolli, Ph.D.
DC Historic Preservation Office
1100 4th Street SW, Suite E650
Washington, DC 20024
Phone: (202) 442-8836
Fax: (202) 741-5246
Email: ruth.trocolli@dc.gov
Visit the D.C. Office of Planning/Historic Preservation Office
at planning.dc.gov/hp

Florida

Mary Glowacki
State Archaeologist and Chief
Bureau of Archaeological Research
Division of Historical Resources
1001 DeSoto Park Drive
Tallahassee, Florida 32301
Phone: (850) 245-6319
E-mail: mglowacki@dos.state.fl.us
Visit the Florida Division of Historical Resources' Bureau of
Archaeological Research at www.flheritage.com

This state SUCKS when it comes to arrowhead hunting laws. There was an excellent isolated finds policy up until 2005. Citizens were allowed to collect on public waterways and voluntarily send in their finds for study, and the artifacts were then returned after one year. After what amounts to a power grab by some horrible state archaeology officials, the isolated finds policy was removed in 2005. These archaeologists used some bad apple artifact hunters as examples and convinced lawmakers to stop all arrowhead hunting on state owned lands and public waterways through new legislation.

I once sent an email to a Florida State Senator complaining about the terrible artifact hunting laws and pointing out that I would not be travelling to Florida as a tourist because of them. The Senator forwarded my complaint to the state archaeologist, who promptly sent me an email stating that I would be arrested if I picked up an arrowhead on a public waterway in Florida. Archaeologists in Florida have successfully grabbed power in the state through these new laws, and they wield it like a club. Avoid Florida if you want to hunt artifacts. In 2010 the Florida Fish and Wildlife Conservation Commission made a total of 14 cases statewide where artifact hunters were arrested, prosecuted, and fined. It is illegal to pick up artifacts on ANY public river or creek in the state of Florida. Surface hunting on private property is OK with landowner permission. The removal of artifacts from state property is punishable with fines and either a first degree misdemeanor or third degree felony, depending on the circumstances, according to Florida Statutes.

Georgia
Dr. Bryan Tucker
State Archaeologist and Section Chief
Georgia DNR-Historic Preservation Division
254 Washington St., SW
Ground Level
Atlanta, GA 30334-9007
404-463-9696
Bryan.Tucker@dnr.state.ga.us
Visit the Georgia Department of Natural Resources Historic Preservation Society

Guam
John Mark Joseph
Territorial Archaeologist
Department of Parks and Recreation
Historic Resources Division
490 Chalan Palasyo
Agana Heights, Guam 96910
Phone: (671) 475-6294

Email: johnmark.joseph@dpr.guam.gov
Visit the Guam Department of Parks and Recreation's Historic Resources Division at ns.gov.gu/dpr/hrdhome.html

Hawaii

Nancy McMahon
Deputy State Historic Preservation Officer
Archaeology and Historic Preservation Manager
State Historic Preservation Division
Department of Land and Natural Resources
Kakuhihewa Building
601 Kamokila Blvd., Suite 555
Kapolei, Hawaii 96707
Ph: (808) 692-8015
Fax: (808) 692-8020
Email: nancy.a.mcmahon@hawaii.gov

Idaho

Kenneth C. Reid
State Archaeologist/Deputy SHPO
State Historic Preservation Office
Idaho State Historical Society
210 Main Street
Boise, ID 83702
Phone: (208) 334-3861
Fax: (208) 334-2775
Email: ken.reid@ishs.idaho.gov
Visit the Idaho State Historical Society's State Historic Preservation Office at www2.state.id.us/ishs/SHPO.html

Illinois

Joseph S. Phillippe

Chief Archaeologist

Illinois Historic Preservation Agency

1 Old Capitol Plaza

Springfield, IL 62701

Phone: (217) 785-1279

Fax: (217) 782-8161

Email: joe.phillippe@illinois.gov

Visit the Illinois State Historic Preservation Agency at www.illinoishistory.gov

Indiana

James Richard Jones III

State Archaeologist/Deputy SHPO

Division of Historic Preservation & Archaeology

Department of Natural Resources

402 West Washington, Room W274

Indianapolis, IN 46204

Phone: (317) 232-1646

Fax: (317) 232-0693

Email: RJones@dnr.IN.gov

Iowa

John F. Doershuk

State Archaeologist

Office of the State Archaeologist

University of Iowa

700 Clinton Street Building

Iowa City, IA 52242-1030

Phone: (319) 384-0751

Fax: (319) 384-0768
Email: John-Doershuk@uiowa.edu
Visit the University of Iowa's Office of the State Archaeologist
at www.uiowa.edu/~osa

Kansas
Bob Hoard
State Archeologist
Cultural Resources Division
Kansas State Historical Society
6425 SW 6th Avenue
Topeka, KS 66615-1099
Phone: (785) 272-8681 extension 268
Fax: (785) 272-8682
Email: rhoard@kshs.org
Visit the Kansas State Historical Society at www.kshs.org

Kentucky
Dr. George M. Crothers
State Archaeologist
W. S. Webb Museum of Anthropology and
Office of State Archaeology
University of Kentucky
1020A Export Street
Lexington, KY 40506-9854
Phone: (859) 257-8208
Fax: (859) 323-1968
Email for Dr. Crothers: gmcrot2@uky.edu
Visit the William S. Webb Museum of Anthropology at
www.uky.edu/AS/Anthropology/Museum/museum.htm

Louisiana
Dr. Charles (Chip) McGimsey
State Archaeologist
Division of Archaeology
1051 North 3rd Street, Room 405
P.O. Box 44247
Baton Rouge, LA 70804
Phone: (225) 342-8170
Fax: (225) 342-4480
Email: cmcgimsey@crt.state.la.us
Visit the Louisiana Division of Archaeology at
www.crt.state.la.us/crt/ocd/arch/homepage/index.htm

Maine
Arthur E. Spiess
Archaeologist
Maine Historic Preservation Commission
65 State House Station
Augusta, ME 04333-0065
Phone: (207) 287-2132
Fax: (207) 287-2335
Email: arthur.spiess@maine.gov
Visit the Maine Historic Preservation Commission at
www.state.me.us/mhpc

Maryland
Maureen Kavanagh
Chief
Office of Archeology
Maryland Historical Trust
Division of Historical and Cultural Programs

100 Community Place
Crownsville, MD 21032-2023
Phone: (410) 514-7600
Fax: (410) 987-4071
Email: mkavanaugh@mdp.state.md.us
Visit the Maryland Historical Trust at
www.marylandhistoricaltrust.net

Massachusetts

Brona Simon
State Archaeologist/Deputy SHPO
Massachusetts Historical Commission
220 Morrissey Boulevard
Boston, MA 02125
Phone: (617) 727-8470
Fax: (617) 727-5128
TDD: (617) 878-3889
Email: brona.simon@sec.state.ma.us
Visit the Massachusetts Historical Commission at
www.state.ma.us/sec/mhc

Michigan

Dean L. Anderson, Ph.D.
State Archaeologist|
SHPO
Michigan State Housing Development Authority
Box 30740
702 West Kalamazoo St.
Lansing, MI 48909-8240
andersond15@michigan.gov
(517) 373-1618

Fax â€" (517) 335-0348
Visit Michigan's Office of the State Archaeologist at
www.michigan.gov/archaeology

Minnesota
Scott Anfinson
Minnesota State Archaeologist
Minnesota Office of the State Archaeologist
Fort Snelling History Center
St. Paul, MN 55111-4061
Phone: (612) 725-2411
Fax: (612) 725-2427
Email: scott.anfinson@state.mn.us
Visit Minnesota's Office of the State Archaeologist at
www.admin.state.mn.us/osa/

Mississippi
Pamela Edwards Lieb
Chief Archaeologist
Department of Archives and History
P O Box 571
Jackson, MS 39205-0571
Phone: (601) 576-6940
Fax: (601) 576-6955
Email: plieb@mdah.state.ms.us
Visit Mississippi's Department of Archives and History at
www.mdah.state.ms.us

Mississippi law for collecting artifacts on public lands is clear.
Mississippi Code 39-7-11 states:

(1) All other sites, objects, buildings, artifacts, implements, and locations of archaeological significance, including, but expressly not limited to, those pertaining to prehistoric and historical American Indian or aboriginal campsites, dwellings, and habitation sites, their artifacts and implements of culture, as well as archaeological sites of every character that are located in, on or under the surface of any lands belonging to the State of Mississippi or to any county, city, or political subdivision of the state, are hereby declared to be Mississippi landmarks and are the sole property of the State of Mississippi. Such sites may not be taken, altered, destroyed, salvaged or excavated without a permit from the board or in violation of the terms of such permit.

State law also makes it illegal to knowingly disturb human remains on private property without a permit from MDAH. In addition, if human remains are encountered, all ground disturbing activity must cease and the Sheriff of the county involved must be notified immediately.

Collecting on private lands

Mississippi gives landowners control of sites on their land, as long as burials are not encountered. You are required to get WRITTEN permission from a landowner and you must carry it with you when hunting.

39-7-31. Entry upon land of another to deface, remove or destroy archeological relics or sites.No person, not being the owner thereof, and without the written consent of the owner, proprietor, lessee, or person in charge thereof, shall enter or attempt to enter upon the lands of another and intentionally injure, disfigure, remove, excavate, damage, take, dig into, or destroy any historical structure, monument, marker, medallion, or artifact, or any prehistoric or historic archaeological site, American Indian or aboriginal remains located in, on or under any private lands within the State of Mississippi. No person without a permit from the board, and without written permission of the landowner, shall intentionally injure, disfigure, remove, excavate, damage, take, dig into, or destroy any prehistoric or historic American Indian or aboriginal burial.

39-7-35. Penalties for violations of chapter; finder's fee for arrest and conviction of violator.

(1) Any person violating any of the provisions of this chapter shall be guilty of a misdemeanor, and upon conviction shall be punished by a fine of not less than five hundred dollars ($500.00) and not more than five thousand dollars ($5,000.00), or by confinement in jail for not more than thirty (30) days, or by both such fine and confinement. Each day of continued violation of any provision of this chapter shall constitute a distinct and separate offense for which the offender may be punished.

(2) The board at its discretion may grant a "finder's fee," not to exceed five hundred dollars ($500.00), for the arrest and conviction of any person in violation of this chapter.

Hunting Arrowheads in Water

Mississippi does not specifically address creek or river hunting of artifacts in its laws. The state grants rights of trespass to stream channels of public waterways, but the disposition of arrowheads found within streambeds remains questionable. It is illegal to DISTURB the bed or bank of a navigable waterway (a waterway big enough for boats).

MISSOURI
Missouri Archaeological Society
Lisa Haney
lhaney@missouristate.edu
PHONE
MAS Office (417) 836–3773
(417) 836–3773Fax
(417) 836–6335
Mail
Missouri Archaeological Society
Missouri State University
901 S. National Ave.
Springfield, MO 65897Fax
Call Lisa Haney in the MAS office. She is helpful and will provide accurate information on state laws.

Awesome laws for hunting arrowheads in Missouri, but state archaeologists are using youtube videos of cave digging to try to get new regulations enacted making all surface hunting on rivers illegal. I DO NOT recommend joining the Missouri Archaeological Society. They are actively trying to make surface hunting illegal. Be aware they will take your money and use it to make your hobby illegal.

Montana
Stan Wilmoth, Ph.D.

State Archaeologist
State Historic Preservation Office
1410 8th Avenue
P.O. Box 201202
Helena, MT 59620-1202
Phone: (406) 444-7719
Fax: (406) 444-2696
Email: swilmoth@mt.gov
Visit Montana's State Historic Preservation Office at
www.his.state.mt.us/shpo

Nebraska
Nebraska State Historical Society
Archeology Division
1500 R Street
P.O. Box 82554
Lincoln, NE 68501
Phone: (402) 471-4789
Fax: (402) 471-3116
Visit the Nebraska State Historical Society's Archeology
Division at www.nebraskahistory.org/archeo/index.htm

Nevada
Rebecca Palmer
Archaeologist, Review and Compliance Officer
State Historic Preservation Office
100 North Stewart Street
Capitol Complex
Carson City, NV 89701
Phone: via Rebecca Palmer (775) 684-3443
Fax: (775) 684-3442

Email: rebecca.palmer@nevadaculture.org
Map: dmla.clan.lib.nv.us/docs/shpo/map.htm
Visit the Nevada State Historic Preservation Office at
www.nvshpo.org

New Hampshire
Richard Boisvert
State Archaeologist
Division of Historical Resources
Department of Cultural Resources
19 Pillsbury St. 2nd Floor
Concord, NH 03301-3570
Phone: (603) 271-3483 or (603) 271-3558
Fax: (603) 271-3433
Voice/TDD: 1-800-735-2964
Email: richard.boisvert@dcr.nh.gov
Visit the New Hampshire Division of Historical Resources at
www.state.nh.us/nhdhr

New Jersey
Karen Flinn
Acting State Archaeologist
Acting Curator, Bureau of Archaeology & Ethnology
New Jersey State Museum
205 West State Street
P.O. Box 530, CN 530
Trenton, NJ 08625-0530
Phone: (609) 292-8594
Fax: (609) 292-7636
Email: karen.flinn@sos.state.nj.us

New Mexico

Glenna Dean

State Archaeologist

Historic Preservation Division

La Villa Rivera

228 East Palace Avenue

Santa Fe, NM 87501

Phone: (505) 827-3989

Fax: (505) 827-6338

Email: gdean@oca.state.nm.us

Visit the New Mexico Office of Cultural Affairs' Historic Preservation Division at museums.state.nm.us/hpd

New York

Christina B. Rieth, Ph.D.

State Archaeologist and Director,

Cultural Resource Survey Program

New York State Museum

Division of Research and Collections,

Cultural Education Center 3122

Albany, NY 12230

Phone: (518) 402-5975

Fax: (518) 486-2149

Email: crieth@mail.nysed.gov

Visit the New York State Museum at www.nysm.nysed.gov/research/anthropology/crsp/

North Carolina

Stephen R. Claggett

State Archaeologist

Office of State Archaeology

4619 Mail Service Center
Raleigh, NC 27699-4619
Phone: (919) 807-6551
Fax: (919) 715-2671
Email: steve.claggett@ncdcr.gov
Visit the North Carolina Office of State Archaeology at
www.archaeology.ncdcr.gov

North Dakota
Paul R. Picha
Chief Archeologist
State Historical Society of North Dakota
Archeology & Historic Preservation Division
North Dakota Heritage Center
612 East Boulevard Avenue
Bismarck, ND 58505-0830
Phone: (701) 328-3574
Fax: (701) 328-3710
Email: ppicha@nd.gov
Visit the State Historical Society of North Dakota at
www.history.nd.gov
Timothy Reed
Research Archaeologist
Historic Preservation Division
State Historical Society of North Dakota (SHSND)
North Dakota Heritage Center
Bismark, ND 58505-0830
Phone: (701) 328-3567
Email: treed@state.nd.us

Ohio

David Snyder
Ohio Historic Preservation Office
800 E. 17th Avenue
Columbus, OH 43211-2474
Phone: (614) 298-2000
Fax: (614) 298-2037
Email: dsnyder@ohiohistory.org
Visit the Ohio Historical Society's Ohio Historic Preservation Office at www.ohiohistory.org/resource/histpres

Oklahoma

Robert L. Brooks
State Archeologist
University of Oklahoma
Oklahoma Archeological Survey
111 East Chesapeake, Room 102
Norman, OK 73019
Phone: (405) 325-7211
Fax: (405) 325-7604
Email: rbrooks@ou.edu

Visit the Oklahoma Archaeological Survey at www.ou.edu/cas/archsur
You can legally surface hunt large federally navigable rivers including the arifact rich ARKANSAS RIVER. Stay out of smaller creeks and streams without landowner permission.

Oregon

Dr. Dennis Griffin
State Archaeologist

State Historic Preservation Office
Oregon Parks and Recreation Department
725 Summer Street, NE, Suite C
Salem, OR 97301-1271
Phone: (503) 986-0674
Fax: (503) 986-0793
Email: dennis.griffin@state.or.us
Visit Oregon's State Historic Preservation Office at
www.oregonheritage.org/OPRD/HCD/index.shtml

Pennsylvania
Kurt W. Carr
Senior Curator of Archaeology
The State Museum of Pennsylvania
300 North Street
Harrisburg, PA 17120-0024
Phone: 717-783-9926
Fax: (717) 214-2990
Email: kcarr@state.pa.us
Visit The State Museum of Pennsylvania at
www.paarchaeology.state.pa.us

Puerto Rico
Balbina Vilar
State Historic Preservation Office
La Fortaleza
Urb April Gardens
c/20 2-f6
Las Piedras, PR 00771
Phone: (787) 447-7779
Email: esenciataina@hotmail.com

Republic of the Marshall Islands
Richard Williamson
State Archaeologist
Historic Preservation Office
P.O. Box 1454
Majuro, MH 96960
Marshall Islands
Phone: 011-692-625-4476
Fax: 011-692-625-4476
Email: rmihpo@ntamar.com

Rhode Island
Charlotte Taylor
Interim Principal/State Archaeologist
Historic Preservation Commission
Old State House
150 Benefit Street
Providence, RI 02903
Phone: (401) 222-4140
Email: charlotte.taylor@preservation.ri.gov

South Carolina
Jonathan Leader
Director/State Archaeologist
South Carolina Institute of Archaeology and Anthropology
University of South Carolina
1321 Pendleton Street
Columbia, SC 29208-0071
Phone: (803) 777-8170 or (803) 734-0567
Fax: (803) 254-1338
Email: leader@sc.edu

Visit the South Carolina Institute of Archaeology and Anthropology at www.cas.sc.edu/sciaa/

South Dakota

James K. Haug
State Archaeologist
Archaeological Research Center
2425 East Saint Charles Street
P.O. Box 1257
Rapid City, SD 57709-1257
Phone: (605) 394-1936
Fax: (605) 394-1941
Email: jim.haug@state.sd.us
Visit the South Dakota State Historical Society's
Archaeological Research Center at www.sdsmt.edu/wwwsarc

Tennessee

Michael C. Moore
Director and State Archaeologist
Tennessee Division of Archaeology
1216 Foster Avenue
Cole Building #3
Nashville, TN 37243
Phone: (615)-741-1588, ext. 109
Fax: (615)-741-7329
Email: Mike.C.Moore@tn.gov
Visit the Tennessee Division of Archaeology at
www.tennessee.gov/environment/arch/

Texas

Patricia Mercado-Allinger

State Archaeologist
Archeology Division
Texas Historical Commission
PO Box 12276
Austin, TX 78711-2276
Phone: (512) 463-8882
Fax: (512) 463-8927
Email: pat.mercado-allinger@thc.state.tx.us
Visit the Texas Historical Commission at www.state.tx.us

Hunting private property with landowner permission is legal in Texas. This is the only state where pay digs are legal. Texas has an official policy making artifact hunting on public waterways illegal, but they do not enforce this policy in practice.

Texas water law is terrible and it's pretty much illegal to float anywhere but on the largest rivers. DO NOT walk around in smaller streams or creeks; you could easily get arrested or even shot dead for trespassing. Do not attempt to hunt Corp of Engineer Lakes in Texas. You will get arrested and fined. These lakes are patrolled by agents looking for arrowhead hunters.

U.S. Virgin Islands

Brooke Persons
Senior Territorial Archaeologist
Virgin Islands State Historic Preservation Office
Fort Frederik
198 Strand Street
Frederiksted, VI 00841

Phone: (340) 719-7089
Fax: (340) 719-8343
Email: BrookePersons@hotmail.com

Utah
Kevin T. Jones
State Archaeologist
Antiquities Section
300 Rio Grande
Salt Lake City, UT 84101
Phone: (801) 533-3524
Fax: (801) 533-3503
Email: ktjones@utah.gov
Visit the Utah Antiquities Section at
http://history.utah.gov/archaeology/index.html

Vermont
Giovanna Peebles
State Archeologist, SHPO and Director
Division for Historic Preservation
National Life Building, 6th Floor
Montpelier, VT 05620-1201
Phone: (802) 828-3050
Fax: (802) 828-3206
Email: giovanna.peebles@state.vt.us
Visit us at http://www.historicvermont.org/

Virginia
Mike Barber
State Archaeologist
Department of Historic Resources

2801 Kensington Avenue
Richmond, VA 23221
Phone: (804) 367-2323
Fax: (804) 225-4261
Email: mike.barber@dhr.virginia.gov
Visit the Virginia Department of Historic Resources at
www.dhr.state.va.us

Washington

Dr. Robert G. Whitlam
State Archaeologist
Department of Community, Trade & Economic Development
Office of Archaeology and Historic Preservation|
P.O. Box 48343
Olympia, WA 98504-8343
Phone: (360) 586-3080
Fax: (360) 586-3067
Email: rob.whitlam@dahp.wa.gov
Visit the Washington State Office of Archaeology & Historic
Preservation at www.dahp.wa.gov/default.htm

Washington state is a VERY anti-collector/hunter environment. This bill was passed by both houses and signed into law in 2011. If you call the state archaeologists you will probably not be well received. It is illegal to hunt public waterways in Washington.

SENATE BILL 5282

State of Washington 62nd Legislature 2011 Regular Session

By Senators Chase, Prentice, Swecker, and Nelson
Read first time 01/20/11. Referred to Committee on
Government Operations, Tribal Relations & Elections.

AN ACT Relating to archaeological investigations on private
land; amending RCW 27.53.030; and reenacting and
amending RCW 27.53.070.

BE IT ENACTED BY THE LEGISLATURE OF THE STATE OF
WASHINGTON:
Sec. 1 RCW 27.53.030 and 2008 c 275 s 5 are each amended
to read as follows:
The definitions in this section apply throughout this chapter
unless the context clearly requires otherwise.

(1) "Archaeology" means systematic, scientific study of man's
past through material remains.
(2) "Archaeological object" means an object that comprises
the physical evidence of an indigenous and subsequent
culture including material remains of past human life
including monuments, symbols, tools, facilities, and
technological by-products.
(3) "Archaeological site" means a geographic locality in
Washington, including but not limited to, submerged and
submersible lands and the bed of the sea within the state's
jurisdiction, that contains archaeological objects.
(4) "Department" means the department of archaeology and
historic preservation, created in chapter 43.334 RCW.
(5) "Director" means the director of the department of
archaeology and historic preservation, created in chapter
43.334 RCW.

(6) "Historic" means peoples and cultures who are known through written documents in their own or other languages. As applied to underwater archaeological resources, the term historic shall include only those properties which are listed in or eligible for listing in the Washington State Register of Historic Places (RCW 27.34.220) or the National Register of Historic Places as defined in the National Historic Preservation Act of 1966 (Title 1, Sec. 101, Public Law 89-665; 80 Stat. 915; 16 U.S.C. Sec. 470) as now or hereafter amended.

(7) "Prehistoric" means peoples and cultures who are unknown through contemporaneous written documents in any language.

(8) "Professional archaeologist" means a person with qualifications meeting the federal secretary of the interior's standards for a professional archaeologist. Archaeologists not meeting this standard may be conditionally employed by working under the supervision of a professional archaeologist for a period of four years provided the employee is pursuing qualifications necessary to meet the federal secretary of the interior's standards for a professional archaeologist. During this four-year period, the professional archaeologist is responsible for all findings. The four-year period is not subject to renewal.

(9) "Amateur society" means any organization composed primarily of persons who are not professional archaeologists, whose primary interest is in the archaeological resources of the state, and which has been certified in writing by two professional archaeologists.

(10) "Historic archaeological resources" means those

properties which are listed in or eligible for listing in the Washington State Register of Historic Places (RCW 27.34.220) or the National Register of Historic Places as defined in the National Historic Preservation Act of 1966 (Title 1, Sec. 101, Public Law 89-665; 80 Stat. 915; 16 U.S.C. Sec. 470) as now or hereafter amended.

(11) "Field investigation" means an on-site inspection by a professional archaeologist or by an individual under the direct supervision of a professional archaeologist employing archaeological inspection techniques for both the surface and subsurface identification of archaeological resources and artifacts resulting in a professional archaeological report detailing the results of such inspection.

Sec. 2 RCW 27.53.070 and 2005 c 333 s 21 and 2005 c 274 s 243 are each reenacted and amended to read as follows:

It is the declared intention of the legislature that field investigations on privately owned lands should be ((discouraged except)) conducted by professional archaeologists in accordance with both the provisions and spirit of this chapter ((and)). Persons having knowledge of the location of archaeological sites or resources are encouraged to communicate such information to the department. Such information shall not constitute a public record which requires disclosure pursuant to the exception authorized in chapter 42.56 RCW to avoid site depredation.

West Virginia
Lora Lamarre
Senior Archaeologist

West Virginia Division of Culture and History
The Cultural Center
1900 Kanawha Boulevard East
Charleston, WV 25305-0300
Phone: (304) 558-0240 extension 711
Fax: (304) 558-2779
Email: lora.a.lamarre@wv.gov

Wisconsin
John H. Broihahn
State Archaeologist
Wisconsin Historical Society
816 State Street
Madison, WI 53704
Phone: (608) 264-6496
Fax: (608) 264-6504
Email: john.broihahn@wisconsinhistory.org

Wyoming
Dr. Mark E. Miller
State Archaeologist
Department of Anthropology
Box 3431 - University Station
Laramie, WY 82071
Phone: (307) 766-5564
Fax: (307) 766-2473
Email: mmiller@uwyo.edu
Visit the Office of the Wyoming State Archaeologist at
http://wyoarchaeo.state.wy.us/

Chapter 5: Finding Indian Camps

Arrowheads are like fish, they travel in schools; where you find one, there will be more. While finding artifacts is the payoff, the real value in any collection is the location of campsites. An expert arrowhead hunter's most prized possession is his site list. If you lost all your arrowheads in a house fire it would be okay, because you still have your site list. You can find more rocks with your site list.

Flint flakes left over from the manufacture of arrowheads are the most obvious sign that you have located an Indian camp. I have found these campsites by not much more than randomly hiking the wilderness. However, hiking around the woods like a drunken lumberjack looking for his keys is not an efficient method of finding Indian camps.

After finding a handful of camps the hard way, I asked myself what these sites had in common, with the intention of using the answer to find more camps. Over time I realized there were 6 things these sites had in common, and that their placement was not random.

Comfortable Outdoor Living

Living outdoors long-term is the same now as it was thousands of years ago. The things you would consider when placing your tent are no different than what an Indian would consider when placing his wickiup. Indians used the same process for the same reasons.

Common Traits of Indian Camps

1.   WATER and FOOD. A human can only live 3 days without water. Your water source can be a creek, river, or spring; preferably the intersection of two waterways. Rivers were the highways and landmarks of their day. River environments contain fish and attract game animals of every size and type. The river was the grocery store of ancient man.

2.   FLOOD PROTECTION. You must camp above the flood plain or you risk death. You might get away with camping low next to the river for a while, but eventually you will be flooded out. Minimum requirements are a high spot next to the river or a first or second tier terrace not far away from water.

3.   WIND PROTECTION. You want storm protection in all directions.   Usually this means there are bluffs, hills, or mountains higher than you and not too far off in the distance. You could camp right next to a bluff or mountain, but only if such an obstacle is to your north.   Wind protection that blocks your sun exposure works against comfortable outdoor living.

4.   SUN EXPOSURE. Long term camps require east, west, and south exposure to the sun, especially the low southern winter sun. You require the sun on your camp from the crack of dawn until dark. It's just plain uncomfortable to camp long term without sun to burn off the morning chill.   Before electricity people were dependent on the sun for light and

warmth, and they could not do much by firelight. It was to their advantage to have sun exposure dawn to dusk.

5. ELEVATION. There are summer camps and winter camps, and the main difference is ELEVATION. Cold air is dense and pools in the valleys. There can easily be a 20 degree difference between campsites in river valleys and campsites halfway up a mountain An Indian moves his camp to take advantage of this temperature difference depending on season. As a general rule, every summertime campsite you find in the river valley has a nearby corresponding winter campsite higher up in elevation.

6. SAFETY and ACCESS. Consider what you would do if you were going to camp outdoors long term with your whole family. Safety and access are important considerations. If you find a great campsite with wind protection and sun exposure, but access to water in the river or spring is down a steep bank, that particular spot would be eliminated from consideration. You need a "walk-up" that is useable for everyone, including small children. A good walk-up should be comfortable enough to use many times every day.

It is very dangerous to camp next to a steep bluff. What if you got up in the middle of the night to "do your business" and accidently walked off the bluff half asleep? Small children might wander off steep cliffs even in the daytime. Many of these spots near bluff edges have good views, but are just plain too dangerous for long term occupation.

I located this camp on a map before leaving the house. This site had footprints on it, but they missed an arrowhead by not checking the gravel well enough. G-9 Table Rock arrow point with a heavily ground base and a needle tip!

My process is to extensively study topographic maps of a new area, and by applying these requirements mark possible camp locations on my map with an X. Then I go check my X's. It's amazing how often it works out. My results are about 50%.

This system has saved me hundreds of miles of random hiking and boating.

Life in the Bowl
A Helpful Construct

For our purposes it is useful to consider ideally located Indian camps as being IN A BOWL. The sides of this imaginary bowl represent wind protection in every direction. In real life the bowl walls are bluffs, mountains, and hills in the distance. This protection should exist 360 degrees around your camp.

The bottom of the bowl is the water level, and you must camp safely above any possible flooding that might wash your camp away, while remaining below the top edge of the bowl to maintain your wind protection. Conceptually we can do this by placing a small rock in the bowl. We would be camping on top of this small rock up out of the flood zone, but still below our wind protection. Not every spot in the bowl will meet your needs. It is important to place the camp rock so it is not shaded by the sides of the bowl at any point during the day.

Rather than constantly reviewing your list of campsite requirements, it will serve you well to picture this bowl while reading maps and while hiking in the field. Mentally superimposing this bowl onto topographic maps and landscapes is a quick and very intuitive way to find these good long-term camping spots. If you find a place where two waterways intersect, and it meets the requirements for placement of the rock in the bowl, you have just located a possible Indian camp. Indian camp locations are based on comfortable outdoor living. You will feel the warmth of full sun and still air while in an Indian camp.

When you find one Indian camp, there will be others nearby. I find camps spaced along rivers at a short distance. Remember that each summer campsite in the river valley will have a corresponding winter campsite in the nearest spot that meets campsite requirements and is 50 feet or more higher in elevation. Finding a one campsite often opens the door to locating others sites. Nearby water sources are not as critical for campsites in winter, there is often snow all around that can be melted for water. I have located long-term occupations on high mountains that are several miles from the nearest running water.

Chapter 6: Arrowhead CSI

Forensic Investigations in Stone

Arrowhead hunting involves many skillsets, including the ability to do detective work. Investigators gather evidence that can help locate the scene of a crime. Our evidence is in the form of flint flakes and camp rocks, and our crime scenes are Indian camps. Evaluation of this evidence requires basic knowledge of the science of stone and techniques of artifact manufacture. Scientific terms are defined below, as well as jargon used by arrowhead hunters. Talking the talk is just as important as walking the walk! Careful reading of this chapter will allow anyone to fake it until they make it.

The Basics of Stone Tool Manufacture

Flint knapping is a very complex subject that I have pared down to essentials. So, without getting too far into the weeds……….

FLINT KNAPPING

Flint knapping is manufacturing rocks into arrowheads, spears, and knives. Hammerstones are used to strike the edge of a rock and remove flakes and spalls. Striking a rock to remove flakes is called Percussion Knapping. Detail work is accomplished by pushing flakes off the edge of a rock with the sharp tip of a deer antler. Pushing flakes off a rock is called Pressure Flaking.

A flint knapper must accurately predict how a rock will break each time he removes a flake. It might take 300 flake removals to shape an arrowhead. Each flake removal requires a separate prediction, decision, and action. A single mistake at any point in the process can destroy the arrowhead. Each complete arrowhead is really a small miracle. While it is not necessary to learn flint knapping, you should watch some knapping videos on the internet to get a good idea of what arrowhead manufacture looks like.

Lithics: of or pertaining to stone. For our purposes lithics refers specifically to types of stone used in making arrowheads. Any stone that fractures conchoidally (con-coyd-alee) can be used to make stone tools.

Conchoidal Fracture: This sounds complicated, but is in fact very simple. If you have ever seen a BB shot into a plate glass window, you have witnessed conchoidal fracture. When a BB is shot into window glass, a small cone of glass is removed opposite the point of impact. This cone shape is the basis for all arrowhead manufacturing techniques. When striking the edge of a piece of flint with a hammerstone, only a portion of that cone is removed.

Nodule: A nodule is a hard mass of minerals, usually rounded, but sometimes "amoeba-like", found in limestone or chalk beds. These nodules of chert or flint are the most common raw material used to make arrowheads. Useful nodules are 3 inches or more, and can be quarried from degraded limestone beds or picked up in rivers and creeks. Supersized nodules allowed the production of 30 inch artifacts, which although rare, do exist in the archaeological record (google DUCK RIVER CACHE).

Chert nodule embedded in limestone on a creek bank.

High quality chert nodule found in the river-8 inches wide.

Flint vs. Chert: There is very little difference between chert and flint, and these words are used interchangeably. The main difference is flint nodules are found in chalk beds, and chert nodules are found in limestone beds. In North America 99% of all nodules will be chert, but 99% of all arrowhead hunters will call them flint nodules.

Indian Campsite Indicators

Man-made flint flakes are the primary indicator of an Indian camp. Being able to tell the difference between a man-made flake and a natural one is a critical skill for an artifact hunter.

My most asked question during the first year was "is this an Indian flint flake?" I asked that same question hundreds of times. I could hand any of my mentors a flint flake and they could tell me if it had been made by an Indian. The funny part is that none of them could tell me how they knew it was Indian-made. They had learned by handling many flakes for years, but did not possess the understanding or terminology for describing why it was an Indian flint flake.

When a hammerstone is used to remove a flake from a rock, a BULB OF FORCE is created. This dome shaped bulb forms when the build-up of force is released all at once by a strike. A bulb of force feels like a small nipple on the face of a flake. This nipple will be round and smooth. It is easy to identify a bulb of force by feel alone. I use my thumb to rub the nipple on a flake, confirming it is man-made. This is not nearly as kinky as it sounds!

A bulb of force indicates a man-made flake. Natural flakes will not have a bulb of force. The "platform" is the spot you strike with the hammerstone. Some flakes will have a platform remnant right next to the bulb of force. Often the platform is broken off when the rock is struck, and no platform will be present. When stone tools are manufactured, many flakes are left lying on the ground in piles. Archaeologists and arrowhead hunters call the leftover flakes from the manufacture of stone tools debitage (deb-ih-taj).

I struck a large flake off this nice piece of dacite with a hammerstone.

The rock was struck in this position with a downward-inward blow.

The dome shape on the flake is the BULB OF FORCE. I took a thick flake to exaggerate the size of the bulb, and make it easier to see. Bulbs of force are proportional to the thickness of the flake,

and thin flakes will have much less pronounced bulbs, more like small nipples.

Cooking Your Rocks: Heat Treatment of Stone

Another clue that you have a man-made flake is heat treatment of the stone. Some rock is good enough to be used in its raw form to produce high quality stone tools. Other times the only rock available is rough, hard, and unsuitable for making nice arrowheads. Low quality rock can be heat treated to improve its workability.

Heat treating was done by burying large flint spalls several inches deep in sand under a fire and cooking them overnight. This thermal alteration results in a more brittle and easily worked stone.   Heat treatment can drastically change the appearance of rock. Dull and chalky becomes colorful and glossy.   Each type of stone changes color and luster differently, and learning what happens to your local stone when heated is important. For example, Burlington chert is a white stone that occurs throughout Missouri, and it varies widely in quality. Low quality Burlington is white and chalky until heat treated, when it becomes pink and lustrous.

In my area, pink lustrous flint flakes indicate they were man-made. Ask an experienced artifact collector about stone types and heat treatment color changes for your area. If you don't know any collectors you can meet some by attending a local Indian artifact show.

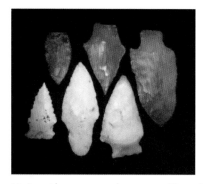

Raw white Burlington chert, same stone heat treated pink.

Arrowhead Hunter's Slang

Using these words correctly will make you instantly "one of the guys" in ANY group of artifact hunters.

Points: Refers to ANY stone tool or artifact with a pointy tip, regardless of whether it was used as a projectile or not.

Pull one out: To find an artifact while hunting. "I am going to try and pull one out." or as a noun "Nice pull!"

Squeak one out: To find a complete artifact in the last few minutes of a hunt. "Glad I was able to squeak one out after hunting all day."

Chunky Monkey: A complete artifact, but crudely manufactured and thick in appearance.

High Grade: Any arrowhead that rates grade 8, grade 9, or grade 10 on the collectors scale. "Found some high grade today!"

Bird Point: This term refers to small arrowheads, some of which are only one quarter inch in length. This is a common term that is completely inaccurate, although everyone uses it anyway! Small arrow points were assumed to have been used to kill small game such as birds. This is not true.

Small arrow points represent the peak of stone projectile technology. These small arrowheads were the "full metal jacket" deep-penetrating bullets of their day. A small stone tipped arrow has the advantage of deeply penetrating game. A "bird point" was much more likely to reach vital organs of game animals.

Even the smallest of these "bird points" were in fact used to kill LARGE game animals such as buffalo and elk, and did a much better job of it than larger, older stone tool technologies. Bird points were also quick to make and required less raw material than larger projectile points.

Smoker: A G9+ artifact that inspires shock and awe. An arrowhead so HOT it SMOKES!

Killer: A G9+ artifact showing high quality manufacture and material.

Hog Sticker: A LARGE artifact. Can be high grade or average. "That's not perfect, but it's a real hog sticker!"

Skunked: To hunt all day and end up with nothing, not even a broke. Once you reach expert level this definition changes. Experts find brokes on every hunt. Skunked for an expert is not finding a complete, undamaged point.

Heartbreaker: A broken artifact that is very well made or large. Not every broken point qualifies as a heartbreaker. Only EXCEPTIONAL broken points are true heartbreakers. But, this term is often used by beginners to describe ANY broken point.

Geo-fact: An odd shaped rock created by nature, but mistaken for an Indian artifact. Some people, especially beginners, think EVERY flake and strange looking rock is an Indian artifact. If you find a rock shaped like a rooster, it is NOT a "chicken effigy." If you find an unusual rock, take it to an experienced hunter or collector and say "I think this might be a geo-fact, what do you think?"

BAD FORM

Don't hold a camp rock or stone knife and say "Look how it fits in your hand. You know it's an Indian artifact when it fits in your hand so well." EVERYONE says that when they first start, it indicates you are a newbie, and its bad form. You could say "this artifact sure is ergonomic" and at least you would be taken seriously.

What is the Difference Between Arrow Points, Dart Points, and Spears?

Three weapon technologies were at play for Indians, and you need to be familiar with all three to understand the difference between arrow points, dart points, and spears.

The simplest technology is a spear. This is a large shaft mounted with a stone point that can be thrust or thrown into game. Spears had a very limited range, and hunting with one was dangerous, as it required an Indian to get close to game. Spear points are larger than dart points or arrow points. This was the earliest weapon technology, but spears were used THROUGHOUT history, right up to historical times. A spear would be a GREAT weapon for up close combat, and could be thrust over and over.

Next was the throwing stick, called an atlatl. An atlatl (rhymes with rattle-rattle) is about 18 inches long, has a handle on one end, and a "spur" on the other. Atlatls acted as an extension of an Indians arm, increasing his leverage, and launched super-sized arrows 4 feet long. These super-sized arrows consisted of a short dart-shaft tipped with a stone point, socketed into a longer shaft with stabilizing feathers. Atlatls are sophisticated technology, and greatly increased range and power while hunting. This increased range allowed safer hunting from a distance, and was a great improvement over a spear.

Dart points are generally larger and heavier than arrow points, because the shafts were longer. Weight of a projectile point is very important, and directly related to the length of the shaft. Longer shafts need heavier points, shorter shafts need lighter, smaller points for proper balance.

This brings us to the bow and arrow, developed last in the line. A bow is a curved piece of resilient wood, with a taut cord tied to each end to propel the arrow. The bow and arrow was superior technology to the atlatl, and eventually replaced it. Bows fire smaller shafts called arrows, and these are tipped with the smallest type of stone projectile, a true arrow point.

By comparing your point's shape to the archaeological record (determining its type) you will know if it's a dart point or an arrowhead. Determining the type of your arrowhead is best accomplished with a regional artifact type guide. Avoid arrowhead type guides that contain prices. Type guides written by archaeologists are far superior to pricing guides.

Use of the bow and arrow dates back 3,000 years in North America, and anything older than that is most likely a dart point. Change does not come easy, and there was some overlap in dart point and arrowhead use. Because of this "inertia of the status quo" there were pockets of Indians still using the atlatl while other tribes had already changed to the bow.

Many arrowheads were used as knives before being used as projectile points. This concept is the Continuum of Reduction. An Indian might not make a projectile from the start. He might make a knife, use it and resharpen it, and when it gets small enough, use it for a projectile. Why do all the work of making a projectile without having the benefit using the tool at its in-between stages?

This reduction continuum would maximize materials and time. I am certain some Indians just made projectiles, but that probably depended on their access to good stone and the amount of time an Indian had available to make stone tools.

Common Objects Found on an Indian Camp

Understanding the shapes, materials, and manufacture of these objects will serve your field investigation skills. Finding more than one of these objects indicates a high probability you are on an Indian camp, and you should search slowly and carefully.

Projectile Point: A stone or bone tool attached to a spear, dart, or arrow shaft.

Top row: 4 dart points. Bottom row: 6 true arrow points.

Right: Handful of drills.

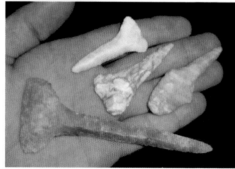

Arrow Point: True arrow points are small enough to be mounted on single piece arrow shafts sized for a bow. Before development of the bow and arrow, stone projectile points were larger and heavier, and mounted on long 2-piece shafts launched by throwing sticks.

Dart Point: Generally larger and heavier than true arrowheads, dart points tipped long 2-piece shafts called darts that were launched by throwing sticks. The main difference between arrowheads and dart points is the length of shaft they were mounted on, and weight, dart points are heavier than arrow points. Darts and throwing sticks pre-date the bow and arrow by 10,000 years.

Drill: These stone tools are long and narrow, like drill bits. Most are between 1 and 12 inches, but are rarely over 3 inches in length. Used projectile points are believed to have been re-sharpened into drills, although some drills are purpose made from the start.

All arrowhead shapes in the archeological record have been found made into drills. Drills are thought to have been used for punching or drilling holes in wood, hide, bone, and stone. Some drills have notched bases for mounting in handles, and some have paddle shaped handles (they look like miniature canoe paddles).

Modern experiments prove these are effective drilling tools. Drills longer than 3 inches were probably not used to drill anything, long drills break during modern experiments. It is speculated that these long drills may have been used to pin clothing together, keep bags closed, or even as hairpins.

Camp Rocks: This term refers to any rock found on an Indian camp that shows use by ancient man. This catch all phrase includes nutting stones, cooking stones, hammerstones, manos, metates, and abrading stones. Under prolonged use, all these tools will eventually break. Broken pieces of these tools are the most common finds on Indian camps, behind flint flakes.

Hammerstone: A round stone used to break pieces off other stones in order to produce stone tools. They come sized from golf balls to grapefruits and every size in between. The size of flake removed depends on the size of the hammerstone. Small stones remove small flakes, and large stones remove large flakes. These stones exhibit peck marks from having impacted the material being worked.

Left: Hammerstones-one grapefruit sized and 2 golf ball sized. Note the obvious peck marks.

Right: Nutting Stones: all three of these nutting stones have indentations from use.

Nutting Stone: A rock used to remove shells from nuts. These stones have at least one flat side, and over time an indentation is created in the flat face or faces. Once shells are crushed and removed, the nut itself is crushed using a different tool called a mano.

Abrading stones have slots and marks.

Abrading Stone: These are rocks with abrasive qualities used for grinding, smoothing, sharpening, or shaping other tools and objects. Abraders are usually made from sandstone. Abrading stones are mainly used to dull edges during flint knapping, and many exhibit grooves from this use.

Cooking Stones: Clay pots and baskets were the only cooking vessels Indians had, and they do not stand up to direct flame. Small round rocks were heated in the fire and dropped into clay pots to boil water. These small round stones are usually 2 or 3 inches in diameter, and often show heat fractures. Eventually, they break apart and pieces of cooking rocks are a common find.

Bi-face: A stone tool flaked on both faces with a sharp edge all the way around. Bi-faces may be oval, triangular, or almond-shaped and represent the basic preform of knives, spears, darts, and arrowheads. Bi-faces may be small or large and are believed to be preforms for later finishing out, although some are finished tool forms used as knives.

Stone Cores: Sometimes a flint knapper's goal is to produce flakes and spalls. These flakes can be used as cutting tools without further modification. Larger thicker flakes (called spalls) are modified further into arrowheads, darts, spear points, and knives. The end result of flake and spall production is a fist sized rock that can have flake scars on every surface, and these are called cores.

Scraper: A stone tool made by chipping the end of a flake or small biface, which is used to scrape animal hides. The steeply angled working edge was used for removing flesh from hides. Hafted scrapers have notches opposite the working end for mounting on handles. Small versions are called thumb scrapers. Thick scrapers with a hump shape are called turtleback scrapers.

Right-Scrapers.

Knife or Spear Point: A knife is a stone blade used for cutting. Knives have two blade faces with a sharp edge on one or both sides. Spear Points are double-edged and symmetrical. Asymmetrical points of any size were probably knives and not projectile points

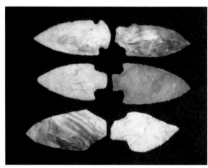

Left: Asymmetrical knives. Lack of symmetry indicates use as a knife.

Right: Spear points or knives.

Large symmetrical double-edged knives and spear points can be used interchangeably. The only difference between a large symmetrical knife and a spear point is the size of shaft they are mounted to. Mount it on a six inch shaft, it's a knife. Mount it on a six foot shaft, it's a spear point!

Some knives are definitely not suitable as projectile points. Some are hand held and can be sharp all the way around. Flake knives are made on flakes with one end dulled as a handle. A knife that has been resharpened many times is called a "depleted knife" and many are often mistaken for projectile points.

A chipped flint axe and a ground stone axe with a full groove.

Axe: A heavy flat cutting tool of chipped or ground stone with a cutting edge on one end. Some axes are meant to be hand held, and some are meant to be mounted at right angles to a handle. The main function of an axe is chopping down trees, but they were also a weapon of war.

Mano: A cylindrical stone shaped like a rolling pin or a flat ovoid, used for grinding and crushing plant material such as acorns, nuts, maize, or pigments.

Manos are ground against a larger bowl shaped stone called a metate and after long use the two stones fit together exactly. Mano/metate combinations are the hallmark of subsistence cultures and are often found on Indian camps where long term occupations took place. Manos are often found alone without a matching metate.

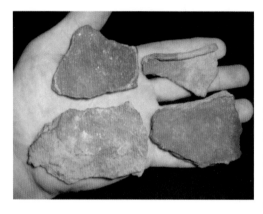

Pot shards, and a rim shard upper right.

Pot Shards: These are pieces of broken pottery vessels. They are tan, brown, red, or black depending on what was type of clay was used to make them and what they were tempered with. In some places these will be very common, and on other sites very rare; either way they are a good indicator of long term Indian occupation.

Chapter 7: Surface Hunting Tools & Techniques

How do you find arrowheads? You walk around and look down. It sounds so simple. Well, maybe it's a little more complicated than that........Surface hunting is accomplished by locating artifacts that have been removed from their original context by natural or man-made erosion. Digging artifacts is a skill, but surface hunting is an ART. Surface hunting is literally rescuing artifacts from certain destruction

Many arrowhead hunters do what I call "ground hog day" style hunting. They pound the same ground year after year using one technique. That's a super formula for ending up with the EVERYMAN COLLECTION; five nice points and 112 not so good ones.

There are many techniques and tools for surface hunting artifacts, and learning multiple methods is a great advantage. I use several methods in combination on most days. Having all these techniques in my arsenal gives me flexibility to recover artifacts regardless of season or conditions. Making proper use of multiple techniques is the difference between a frame of high grade points and a coffee can of chunky monkeys.

Plowed Field Hunting
Hunting plowed fields is an American tradition going back to the first settlers. The first farmers to plow fields were rewarded with an amazing bounty of Indian artifacts. I found

an early settler's diary entry that said "Plowed the low field in the river bottom today, found 200 arrowheads." Indian artifacts were a curiosity that held no monetary value in those days. Arrowheads were thought of as a nuisance by some, who were afraid the sharp rocks might injure their livestock while plowing. Many fine arrowheads were used as skipping rocks and thrown into rivers. One farmer wrote "The long ones skip the best." Ever since reading that, I have been plagued by visions of an old time farmer throwing 4 inch Clovis points into the river.

From the standpoint of personal safety, plowed field hunting is the safest way to recover arrowheads. People die every year attempting to find arrowheads. Rivers and lakes are dangerous places compared to plowed fields. If you fall down while hunting a plowed field, you will get dirty, but the only thing hurt will be your pride! This type of hunting is the most appropriate for bringing children along.

Crops still get planted right where Indian campsites are located. When these fields get plowed artifacts are exposed. Not every plowed field will contain artifacts, but any plowed field near a waterway is worth checking out. The first thing you need is permission from the landowner.

Landowner Permission

Get permission from a landowner before hunting a plowed field. Without permission you will be trespassing and stealing from a landowner. Obtaining permission can be as easy as driving up to the farmhouse nearest to the field and asking. If you are not at the right house, you will usually be directed to it.

Sometimes when you find yourself at the wrong house, a landowner's neighbor might be an arrowhead hunter; he may try to throw you off by telling you something like "That's old man Johnson's field, and you can go ask him, but he ain't real sociable and you might get shot." or "That's not my land, but Mr. Jones don't like arrowhead hunters on his land." I don't know what makes some people want to exert their influence over other people's property, but this happens FREQUENTLY. Don't be fooled. Keep trying houses and you will eventually find the real landowner.

First impressions are everything and if you don't look right and talk right you can pretty much forget about it. If the landowner collects arrowheads, it's over right there. Some landowners actually post signs that say "NO ARROWHEAD HUNTING" although this is relatively rare.

Keep it direct and simple, and if you look like some long-haired hooligan you will get nowhere. If you are wearing your hat, take it off and hold it in your hand.

Your conversation might go something like this: "my name is _____ and I live in _____. My hobby is hunting arrowheads and I noticed your plowed field here by the river. Would it be ok for me to walk around and look for some arrowheads?"

Most landowners are worried about liability and damage to their crops. You are more likely to get permission in fresh turned dirt with no crops planted. If there are plants in the field be careful to step between rows, DO NOT STEP ON CROPS. Don't litter and be sure to pick up any trash you find. If a landowner agrees to let you hunt, you will be expected to ask permission every time you come. I have developed many good relationships over the years, and eventually you will get the landowner's phone number and be able to call ahead and ask.

If you hunt a field often and are enjoying yourself finding points, it's good to give the landowner something once in a while. A turkey around Thanksgiving or a ham at Christmas is a good idea. Once you are in good with a landowner, BE CAREFUL WHAT YOU SAY ABOUT YOUR FINDS. If the landowner gets the impression you are finding a bunch of really great valuable points, you might see your permission rescinded.

Show them your finds if they ask, but not that 5 inch dovetail valued at $2,000 (that's not going to happen, but if it does KEEP QUIET). Don't bring other people unless it's your child, most farmers won't mind you bringing your boy or girl along.

Most fields have been plowed for a hundred years, and many artifacts will be damaged by farm machinery. However it is still possible to find some pretty nice stuff in plowed fields.

In the past EVERY field got plowed for weed control purposes. This wide-spread plowing of land ended a few years ago when some horrible man invented a thing called "no-till farming." This type of farming uses chemicals instead of plowing to control weeds for hay crops. Because hay is the most common crop produced (farmers need hay to feed livestock) this means NOT MANY FIELDS get plowed these

days. The proliferation of no-till farming has definitely reduced the amount of artifacts recovered in modern times.

A just-turned field will produce flint flakes and maybe an artifact or two, but for best results you need rain on the dirt. Fresh turned dry dirt hides artifacts from view and rocks tend to sink into dry dust.

Plowed Field Action
December 2010
Hunt Report

December can be a difficult month to find points. Between the weather and the holidays getting in the way it's tough to pull one out. Three days ago it snowed 11 inches over a 5 county area. It never crossed my mind that snow could somehow HELP me recover points. Snow on the ground usually means digging is the only option. But this snowstorm proved helpful in a way I had never imagined.......

The day after the 11 inch snowfall, temperatures rose to near 40 degrees and the sun was beaming all day. Most of the snow melted off and the ground was very wet. This set the stage for a truly amazing event. The next day a massive rainstorm settled over a quarter of the state. Overnight temperature remained above freezing, and I knew this could mean some killer erosion.

I watched the rainfall totals rise on the national weather service map with great anticipation. One, two, and then three inches; best of all it was right on top of an awesome hunting spot. I knew the field had been plowed for weed control and was fallow. Because of the snow melt the day before, I figured it was a swamp in that plowed field. Although the field was 38 miles away, technology allowed me to know what was going on there. I did not need to call ahead for permission. I had already been given free access by the landowner due to the fallow condition of the field.

It was 35 degrees with a light rain the next morning. I was wearing big hiking boots and geared up for cold weather. My wildest dreams could not have prepared me for the sight of that field. It looked like World War One trench warfare. Normally I would wait several days for a field to firm up, so I could avoid walking in six inch deep muck. Today I decided to strike while the iron was hot.

Pretty nice handful of points!

I took off into the field at a snail's pace, each step a labor from the weight of mud that instantly built up on my boots. Fortunately I know the location of every hot spot in the field from having hunted it before. I found a fallen tree branch along the edge of the field, and prepared a 4 foot flipping stick in a matter of minutes. I began finding lots of broken points right away. I was finding more brokes than my pockets could hold. Pockets bulging, I spotted two whole points in close succession. Then I found a killer pink table rock stemmed to round out the day, and hiked out with my treasure.

My thighs were burning from 3 hours of hiking in the muck. That mud gets pretty heavy on my boots and lifting extra weight with every step wears me out fast. I ended up with 34 broken points and 3 pretty nice, complete, undamaged arrowheads.

Willy B.

Flipping Sticks

Use a "flipping stick" to turn over every piece of flint showing, no matter how small. Rain will often expose only a tiny part of an arrowhead, and by flipping them out will you know if it's a flint flake or an artifact. Flipping sticks keep you from having to bend over 300 times per hunt, which saves your back a lot of work. Flipping sticks are a necessity. You will become quickly worn out from bending over to check flakes without a good flipping stick.

Some hunters make their own flipping sticks from wooden handles with a small nail driven into the tip. This allows them to use the nail to flip flint easily. My personal method is "field expediency" and I look around for a four foot stick on site. If you break this stick with a branch juncture at the end it works the same as the "nail in the end of a broken hoe handle" technique.

If it's not an artifact, leave it be and keep looking. If you pick up a flint flake for any reason, it's a good idea to put it in your pocket and pack it off the field. This saves you double work flipping the same flakes rain after rain. It's not practical to pick up all the flakes, but you shouldn't drop them back down either.

Hunting Fields with Crops in Them

Some fields are so good it's worth hunting them with mature crops growing. Wait for several inches of rain to hit a field before attempting this. Rain is the RESET button and will expose new artifacts. You will probably only get this type of permission if you already have a good relationship with a landowner. Crops are literally the bread and butter on a farmers table, and if you step on their crop you are costing them money.

One last warning for you city slickers, messing around in a farmer's field without permission, especially with crops planted, is a good way to get shot. Don't do it. You could easily end up as corn fertilizer.

Step carefully between rows of planted crops. It is possible to hunt effectively with 10 foot high corn in a field, but the corn leaves are very sharp, and will cut you or poke your eye if you don't move slowly and carefully. The biggest problem with high corn is that you will get lost.

Keeping your bearings in a high corn field takes planning. The best method is to plan your route BEFORE entering high corn. Get your bearings while you can still see landmarks, and walk in one direction to your planned exit point. Repeat this each time you go into the corn.

How to Walk a Field Effectively
Enter a plowed field with a plan. Walk lines about 6 feet apart back and forth. I call it "mowing the lawn." Keep your focus on a small area, scanning about 3 feet to your left and right. Your own footprints will tell you where you have already been. Flip all flint that you see with your stick, no matter how small it appears. It is surprising how often a small exposure of flint turns out to be an artifact. Many times only tiny pieces of tips, ears, and edges are exposed.

Certain areas of every field will contain concentrations of flint flakes and artifacts. These "hot spots" represent heavily occupied areas. All hot spots should be double hunted by retracing your initial path, but in the reverse direction. It is amazing what you can miss on just one pass through, and things look very different from a different direction.

Often I am not the first person to walk plowed dirt. Do not be discouraged by the presence of footprints on a field. Many times I have found points missed by other hunters, sometimes inside their own prints! Concentrate on areas between footprints and try to walk the opposite direction of any footprints you see.

You will get the best results hunting a plowed field after a rain, but ideally you should wait a couple of days after a good thunderstorm for the ground to dry and firm up. It adds a lot of difficulty when you hunt immediately after the rain. The mud weighs down your feet and slows you down. However, if there is competition in a particular field, go hunt in the mud anyway. Be first if you want the good stuff!

If a particular field gets REALLY heavy pressure, there are ways to beat the crowd. I once counted 16 people hunting a single field at the same time! This particular field is so rich with artifacts, that more than one person shows up at the crack of dawn the morning after a good rain. Knowing this, a few of us show up at 3 am and hunt with headlamps. When hunting at night you are best served by sticking to the heavily occupied hot spots on the field.

River Bottom Hunting
Finding Arrowheads in Water

For thousands of years arrowheads have been deposited into rivers. They erode from cut-banks that were once Indian camps. Many artifacts are sitting on the bottom of creeks and rivers, waiting for someone to pick them up. But they don't stay there forever. Moving water pushes arrowheads downstream with all the other rocks. As they travel they get damaged and eventually destroyed.

You have a lot better odds of finding an artifact in the water than sticking out of a cut-bank. The reason for this is that most times when an arrowhead is eroded from a bank nobody is there to pick it up and it washes into the river. The more damage an artifact found in the water shows, the farther it has traveled. If you find an undamaged crispy sharp point in the water, look up. You are below an Indian camp, and that undamaged point just fell into the water.

It is amazing how some artifacts survive surfing the gravel bars, in spite of the odds. A river point can be banged up all the way around its edge and still exhibit an impressive beauty and character. Many creek and river points show stain from tannic acid. Tannic acid is created when leaves fall into the water and dissolve. The water becomes rusty brown and stains the arrowheads giving them what is referred to as "creek stain." In slow moving river systems that have a lot of sand, the artifacts get a high sand-polish much sought after by collectors.

Begin by searching the creek or river bottom below high cut-banks. Many high spots next to the river were once summertime Indian camps. If the water below these cut-banks is slow moving and shallow, it's possible to just walk along and look at the bottom right through the water. You will be able to see artifacts through several feet of water in some locations.

Look for tips, ears, points, and edges, as well as full outlines and the texture of knapped flint. Some artifacts will be laid out on the bottom fully exposed.

This simple technique works fine as long as there is no breeze making ripples on the surface that block your view. Fast moving water will also keep you from being able to see the bottom. There is a way to look through wind rippled water, as well as rapids.

Underwater Viewers

Underwater viewers are windows to an invisible world. I didn't make my first viewer until my second year, after I watched an old timer using a glass pie dish to see the bottom of the river. He would tote it around in his backpack. It was heavy, breakable, and too shallow, often being overtopped by waves. I watched him struggle to hold the pie plate as he bent over for hours. I recognized the genius of the concept, but knew there was a better way. I began designing and building my own viewers the next day.

This is my single most powerful tool for river hunting. Most people look at these and think "well that is simple and obvious." It's easy to think something is simple and obvious once you watch someone else do it. It was not obvious to me, and certainly construction of a high end viewer is anything but simple.

Designing your own viewer is half the fun. There is no set design, use whatever is available that works for you. Designing and building artifact hunting tools is a hobby within the hobby for me. One of my buddies used a hard foam bait bucket with an acrylic sheet glued inside. It worked like a charm. I have also seen a store bought clear plastic dry goods containers (the type with vacuum lids) used to great effect!

My first viewer consisted of a five gallon bucket with the bottom cut out and an acrylic sheet glued inside. These work well and can even be bought online for about $30. After a while I became tired of toting around a 5 gallon bucket and looking through scratched up plastic. If you use a viewer 50 days a year "disposable" designs just won't get the job done. The redesign and improvement process begins out of necessity.

I think of my viewer like a soldier thinks of his weapon. Many times I would have returned home empty- handed without an underwater viewer. Because this tool produces results, I am willing to spend money on the best materials and time on the best design. Construction of my latest model viewer is one part hillbilly ingenuity, one part material analysis, and one part mechanical engineering.

The ideal viewer has clear sides that allow the sun to pass through and illuminate the bottom. Holding a viewer for hours causes your hands to cramp up, but a good neck strap alleviates this. I have 9 different viewer designs, each an improvement on the last. I currently use one of 3 different designs to get the best result in a given situation.

My 8th generation viewer design is a 12 inch high by 10 inch wide butyrate plastic tube. I use 1/8 inch thick window glass cut to fit the end. Butyrate is a special plastic that can be cut and drilled with woodworking tools. Acrylic tubes will split and shatter if you try to drill or cut them.

Right: My 8th Generation viewer. Silicone seals the glass to the end of the tube, but silicone alone won't hold the glass, so I mounted a rubber bumper taken from a large spotlight to hold the

glass in place. The bumper offers impact resistance on the vulnerable edges. Window glass offers a better view and won't scratch up like plastic.

Super triangular knife found in 2 feet of water below a dam.

My 9th Generation floating viewer and a point I just spotted.

My floating viewer uses the hood from an air oven "as seen on tv." The clear plastic hood is 13 inches wide and 8 inches deep. I use the air oven hood upside down, with the wider part UP so it floats on the surface without being overturned by waves. Because it floats like a boat, I don't have to hold it. This viewer uses scratch resistant ¼ inch thick lexan instead of glass for its window. By using special 2 part structural glue used for aquarium construction, no other parts are required in the assembly! Simply glue the lexan to the oven hood. Underwater viewers work really well and allow you to hunt in places where other hunters can't see. My floating viewer is easier to use than previous designs, because you don't have to hold it.

If you spot an artifact in 2 feet of water in the winter time, you will have difficulty getting the point off the bottom. It's too cold to reach in, and you end up getting your clothing wet. I have seen small bait nets with a 2 foot handle used for retrieving underwater artifacts in winter. Another hunter uses a large plastic serving spoon attached to a 3 foot handle. I often use my paddle to fish out an arrowhead from deep water in the winter.

Deep Water Point Retrieval
March 2009

We had been river hunting 3 hours when my buddy spotted it. An arrowhead was lying in the middle of a crystal clear pool. The problem was he would have to get through 4 feet of COLD water to get it. It was 40 degrees and not a good day to go underwater. We tried retrieving it with our paddles to no avail. It was just too far out. The point sure looked nice sitting on the bottom. We had waterproof bags in our boats with a full change of clothing and even towels to dry with.

I looked at him and said, "How bad do you want that arrowhead?" He wanted it, but maybe not bad enough to go swimming in March. It looked really nice. I told him if he didn't want it, I would go in and get it. He replied hopefully "And you will give it to me?" I said "No. I don't think so. It will be mine if I go into this cold water to get it."

My buddy didn't seem too happy at this point. If it turned out to be a G9 hog-sticker, he would really feel bad at not having retrieved it. Although it was 90 percent exposed, the only way to know for sure was to PUT YOUR ENTIRE BODY underwater on a 40 degree day.

Decision made, he stripped down to his boxers. After he hesitated for a few seconds, I said "Make it quick, you are just prolonging the agony." He screamed as he entered the water. He screamed again as he approached waist level. A few seconds later the deed was done, and the point was retrieved.

It was missing an ear. I tried not to laugh, but it didn't work.

The next time we went river hunting, he brought a rubber dip net with a long telescoping handle. There was no way he was ever doing that again, but he wasn't going to leave any points in the water either. Years later I noticed that one-eared point in his frame. Turns out the story that went with it made it one of his favorite finds!

Happy Hunting
Willy B.

Getting Results with an Underwater Viewer
Following the Flood

While viewers will work any time, there is one more important consideration. Moss grows on the rocks under water and then it becomes MUCH more difficult to see any artifacts. The secret here is to hunt in the 3 or 4 day window after the river recedes from rain flooding, but before the moss has a chance to grow back.

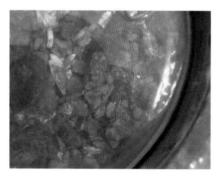

G9 Table Rock Stemmed covered in moss, making it difficult to spot. This point would have been invisible in a couple more days!

Once again TIMING IS EVERYTHING. When the river rises after a good rain, the rain flood TURNS OVER ALL THE ROCKS and removes the moss. This turnover of the rocks is the key to successfully recovering artifacts from under the water with a viewer.

You know what's happening to water levels from a distance by watching the United States Geological Survey real time water data website. This taxpayer funded system places remote gauges in every river in your state. These gauges give current water levels in REAL TIME, and are a valuable resource for finding arrowheads. You could have the best viewer ever built and know every camp on the river, but if you don't get your timing right chances are you won't even find a flake.

Bank Hunting: Finding the Bank of Origin

Finding points in the water is great, but if you want to improve the quality of your finds, you need to get them BEFORE they fall into water and become damaged. If you can locate the bank of origin, you can find arrowheads as crispy and sharp as the day they were made.

The more damage an artifact shows generally the farther it has traveled; if you find an undamaged crispy point in the water YOU ARE AT THE BANK OF ORIGIN. Now you know to check the bank RIGHT THERE after the rain floods.

Once you find a mostly undamaged artifact in the water, turn and face upstream. There should be high cut-banks within sight for this technique to work. Cut-banks produce a hundred flint flakes for every artifact, and there will be a trail of flint flakes heading downriver from a good bank. You are looking for flint flakes in the water.

Search slowly and carefully. Keep going until you stop finding flakes. The cut-bank to your right or left is probably the bank of origin. Search this bank carefully for flakes, camp rocks, and arrowheads. If you don't find anything, don't be discouraged. Remember that exact spot on the bank and check it after every flood.

Patience is the key in locating banks of origin. You might not find the origin bank on the first try. It often takes me several visits after rainstorms to find the sweet spot. Cut-banks do not constantly dump flakes and points, be patient. One of my best regularly hunted banks produced no flint or artifacts for 5 months.

Found it! Flint flakes in their original deposition on a creek bank. The tool is a stainless steel cheese-knife/bottle-opener!

Fire Pits: A Dead Giveaway

Pictured above is a fire pit in the bank of a small creek. Fire pits are stained lines and lens shaped areas darker than the surrounding soil in a cut-bank wall. These deposits were once fires burned by ancient Indians. You will often find charcoal, flint flakes, and even arrowheads contained in these features.

I had to build some steps by stacking rocks to reach this artifact. In the summer sun-dried cut-banks will be as hard as stone. You will need to soften them up with water in order to remove any artifacts sticking out.

This point would not budge even after half way digging it out!

Finally dug it out, a crispy undamaged Smith, one ear sharpened off, but sharp as the day it was made.

Fire pits can be up high near the grass line or way down low by the water line. The farther below the grass line the older the deposit, and the better your chances of finding older point types. Don't limit yourself to just looking for fire pits. Look everywhere, especially once you find an artifact or worked flake.

Be extra careful when looking down a cut-bank from above as they can give way and you can go with them. Falling off a cut-bank of even 6 or 8 feet can kill you. You can stack large rocks and use them as steps to reach an artifact from below.

My other piece of advice is once you find a good bank don't tell anyone else. A single good bank well hunted can furnish you with high grade artifacts for the rest of your life. My highest quality finds are obtained this way. Even digging doesn't produce as many finds of this quality because there is no chance of chipping an artifact with your digging tool if you spot it sticking out of a cut-bank.

Creeking

Creeking is the favorite and only method of some artifact hunters. This is a great entry level technique because it requires no equipment. Creeking is like river hunting, but on a smaller scale. You will not need a boat, because most creeks aren't big enough to float a kayak. Hike the creek and search the banks and bottom.

Not all creeks will contain artifacts, but any creek is worth giving the once over. It can take years to figure out which creeks produce artifacts, but creeks that occur in ecological transition zones are more likely to contain artifacts. Ecological transition zones are where two different types of environments meet. This can be mountains to prairies, prairie to forest, upland forest to lowland forest, etc. Ecological transition zones are marked by changes in vegetation and altitude.

Concentrate your hunting where springs enter a creek, and where creeks enter the river (anywhere two waterways meet). High banks on the creek should get special attention. Everything is on a smaller scale on creeks, so cut-banks even 6 feet high are considered high spots. Once you find a flint flake or an artifact SLOW DOWN and look very carefully.

Rain floods the creeks on a much smaller scale; it depends on the total length of the creek drainage. Creeks over ten miles long can flood enough to turn the gravel over like on the bigger rivers, and when the rocks get turned over you will get the best results.

This method is great in the summer, but even better in the winter. However, you will need some gear to hunt creeks in the winter. Knee high rubber boots or neoprene chest waders are essential if you want to hunt a creek in cold weather. Cold weather eliminates most competition, and brings on the freeze/thaw cycle. Creek banks will drop large chunks of soil into the water as the temperature fluctuates above and below 32 degrees, causing bank soil to expand and contract. Sometimes these chunks of soil contain artifacts. Once enough water washes over these chunks, artifacts contained within are released into the creek. Although it seems counter-intuitive, more erosion occurs in the winter from the freeze/thaw cycle than from flooding.

An underwater viewer allows you to view the bottom of a creek where water is moving fast or windy conditions create ripples that block your view. Don't forget to hunt the banks of the creek as well, that's where the artifacts are coming from. If you find an undamaged crispy arrowhead in the water, check the banks closely, you are at the bank of origin.

In small creeks consider sifting the gravel below cut-banks that produce artifacts. There are often high concentrations of artifacts in the creek bottom gravel. Small creeks do not flood on the same scale as rivers with large drainages, and consequently the artifacts are not always washed away. In small creeks you can shovel the gravel from the creek bottoms into a floating sifter, or a milk crate turned upside down. A single upside down milk crate works great in shallow water, if the water is deeper use two crates stacked. Shovel the creek bottom gravel right onto the top of the upturned milk crate. Search the gravel for artifacts and dump the rocks to the side.

Be sure to get landowner permission for creek hunting. Creeks too small for a kayak and spring branches are private property.

Grubbing

Grubbing arrowheads is a technique that seems crazy at first, but you will be amazed at how well it works. When creek and river bank campsites erode they slump large chunks of soil into the river. These chunks of soil become mud. This mud contains flint flakes, camp rocks, and artifacts. Once the river floods, the mud is washed away revealing any artifacts.

Instead of waiting for this slump mud to be washed away by the river currents, you are going to take a shortcut. You are going to reach right down into that mud and feel around for arrowheads! There is no point in grubbing unless you are below cut-banks of known Indian camps or at least cut-banks that show lots of flint flakes falling out of them. Grubbing the mud below high banks is effective on big rivers and tiny creeks alike.

Noodling Arrowheads
August 2009

Some call it hillbilly hand fishing, and some call it noodling. I call it just plain crazy. You float around in the river searching the riverbanks for underwater holes. Some of these holes contain large catfish. The idea is to use your hand for bait by reaching into the hole. If there is a large fish in the hole, it will bite your hand, and at that point you grab the fish and pull it out.

This is an aboriginal fishing technique, and probably derived from being very hungry. It takes courage to feel around underwater in dark holes, but hunger can easily overcome fear. Modern humans do this for the rush. Noodling has the same rush as rattlesnake hunting. Time slows down and you feel your mortality. There is no better way to feel alive than to face your fear. It takes a lot of nerve to stick your hand in that hole, more than you can imagine if you haven't tried it.

Noodling arrowheads is not quite as crazy as noodling 50 pound catfish, but it does take some nerve. A friend of mine has been hunting one particular creek for many years now. He knows this creek well and has located an Indian camp along the bank. This creek bank has flint flakes falling out of it, and sometimes artifacts.

We had hunted the creek bottom below this bank and found a couple of brokes, but nothing really good. My buddy then proceeded to sit on his knees in about a foot of mud and water directly under this same bank. He reached in with both hands and started feeling around. I stood in the creek behind him, watching incredulously. No way I was gonna do that. That's just plain crazy. Who knows what's in that mud waiting to bite you?

After about 5 minutes, without turning around to face me, without saying a word, he raised his right arm into the air. Between his thumb and index finger was a 4 inch black spear point. It took me all of 5 seconds to jump down in that slump mud and start feeling around with both hands.

It's amazing how all fear disappears once somebody finds a nice arrowhead!

Willy B.

This is a warm weather only technique and you will get wet and muddy. You will be tempted to wear gloves when doing this. But if you want the best results use your bare hands. Bare hands allow you much better feel. Although flint is sharp it's relatively rare to cut your hands. Move your hands slowly and deliberately through the mud. At the lake I have grubbed up broken glass and fish hooks with my bare hands, but rarely get cut. There isn't any difference between broken glass and flint flakes as far as sharpness.

Grubber Warning

NEVER grub in warm stagnant water. Standing water contains parasites and bacteria. If you had an open cut or accidentally got cut while grubbing stagnant water you could end up with a life threatening infection. Many people have lost fingers and legs from parasitic flesh eating bacteria. Avoid heavily polluted rivers and slow moving warm water. If you get cut and it gets infected, visit a doctor immediately. Some people get an infected cut after being in the river and think it will just go away. They don't see a doctor right away, and end up losing a limb. That's a high price to pay for being a tough guy. Apply antibiotic ointment on any cuts you get as soon as possible. If your cut turns bright red or you see red lines radiating from it, SEE A DOCTOR IMMEDIATELY.

Grubbing is also effective technique on submerged lake sites.

Lake Hunting

The internet is a generally not a good place for arrowhead hunting advice. Lots of people will publish hunting tips on the internet, and most of them have no idea what they are talking about. I was advised on one website to "look for natural lakes because man-made lakes weren't around in Indian times and you won't find arrowheads on the shoreline." In reality, nothing could be further from the truth. Internet arrowhead hunting advice is so bad it offends my sense of right and wrong, and was one of my motivations for writing this book.

You will find many Indian campsites on the lakeshores of man-made lakes. The key to hunting man-made lakes is locating the river channel that is now submerged below the water. Use your topographic map and locate this river channel. When the submerged river channel coincides with a submerged terrace, these terraces are likely Indian camps. Some of these terraces are high enough to be exposed when lake levels drop. Wind and wave action expose artifacts on these terrace campsites.

Once a terrace camp is submerged, the topsoil is literally melted off. This leaves a layer of sand on top of a hardpan clay layer. This layer of sand contains flint flakes, camp rocks and artifacts. Grubbers reach into this sand layer, and feel around for arrowheads.

After lake levels drop wave action and rain wash the sand away, leaving flint flakes, camp rocks and artifacts laid out on the clay hardpan. If you can locate a recently exposed terrace camp chances are you will find arrowheads.

Drought and Dropping Water Levels

Over time you will get to know your lake's normal level. When lake levels drops during times of drought many new campsites will be exposed and eroded by wave action. You can find artifacts on these camps once they are exposed. A good rain on these sandy exposed terraces is like hitting a "reset button". Rain obliterates footprints and exposes new artifacts.

Lake grubbing occurs on terrace sites that are still submerged in 1 to 3 feet of water. Once a site is exposed to air, the sand packs too tightly for grubbing. Hunt submerged sites by floating over them, reaching down into the sand and feeling around for artifacts. It's a little scary but you can find some really good stuff.

This technique is great for beginners. You can take groups of people to known sites and even inexperienced grubbers will find artifacts. This is especially fun on 100 degree days, when other types of hunting are not possible. If you have a designated driver, a cooler full of beer and some BBQ won't hurt either!

Some people use floating sifters and a shovel for this type of hunting, but this can draw unwanted attention, bringing competition from others on the lake. If you have no digging or sifting equipment, nobody will figure out what you are doing. Once you tell other people what you are up to, they will join in or come back after you leave. Competition is not something you want. Don't tell anyone what you are doing on the lake. You will regret it the next time you come down and ENTIRE FAMILIES are grubbing your spot!

Surf Zone Hunting

Surf zones occur anywhere waves and shorelines meet. The wave action erodes shorelines constantly. Areas where the slope of a beach is gradual create the best erosion. These active surf zones occur on lakeshores, riverbanks, and ocean beaches. An Indian camp in an active surf zone can literally be hunted every day, because it gets constant erosion, which reveals more flint flakes, camp rocks and artifacts. However, there are certain times when surf zone hunting is much better. After a good storm beaches will be primed for hunting. When water levels drop new areas become active surf zones, and produce many artifacts.

WINTER SURFING
December 2012

I am primarily a surface hunter, and surface hunting is erosion driven. Wave action produces some fine erosion, and is pretty much continuous on submerged lake campsites. These camp soils were originally composed of dirt, sand, and a deeper underlying layer of clay.

Lake water causes dirt to melt away, leaving a layer of sand filled with camp rocks, flint flakes, and artifacts. Grubbers reach into this sand and feel around for artifacts, but you can't grub on a 35 degree December day!

A lot of topsoil has melted away, this stump indicates the soil level before the lake was flooded.

The lake dropped a foot since my last visit. The last window for arrowhead hunting was a 60 degree sunny day a few days before Christmas. Since then it's been cold. 15 degree lows and 35 degree highs. This leads me to believe nobody has been hunting these sites for the last week. Today I planned on hunting BASS ISLANDS. Bass Islands consists of 2 islands about 100 yards apart.

Cold weather doesn't mean jack if you gear up properly. In the winter neoprene chest waders, a wind breaker, and my lucky stocking hat keep me plenty warm.

The wind was forecasted to gust 12 mph, and that is near my 15 mph limit, so I would have to be extra careful and pull my kayak ALL THE WAY UP onto the islands. If you don't tie up your boat or pull it completely out of the water, it can be *blown away and leave you stranded. I would be paddling just under 3 miles total to get to these two islands and back.*

I drove to the lake and hit the water at my planned time of noon. Temperatures would rise to 35 degrees by noon, a tolerable level. Anything below 35 degrees on a windy day, and you will be miserable. Today I was at my working limit for wind and temperature. This would give me only 5 hours to hunt. After sunset temperatures drop off quickly, and dark comes at 5:05.

A brisk paddle of 1 1/2 miles kept me warm all the way. It looked very prime. I noticed the beach was smooth, indicating no one had been here recently. I smiled.

Flakes were freaking EVERYWHERE. It wasn't 10 minutes before I was taking my first in-situ. Looked like a possible bird point. I was using a flipping stick, a beaver chew about 4 feet long I had brought with me. I found several brokes, and then took another in-situ photograph. I worked my way around the tip of the site, picked up several more brokes, and took another in-situ.

I had been paying special attention to the surf zone at first, because there was only a slight breeze. If the wind picks up, you can't see through the water surface. The wind had now kicked up to about a steady 10 mph and the surf zone was no longer visible, so I concentrated on the 4 feet of new beach exposed by recently dropping lake levels.

I finished up on the first island and paddled over to the second one. WOW, awesome amount of flint and camp rocks. In the first minute I had flipped up a nice point, and spotted a whole point fully exposed

When a point is sticking up like this we call it "tombstoned."

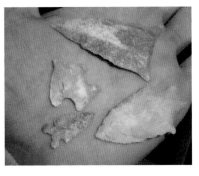

The arrow point is nice (bottom left). The white point (bottom right) is complete, but it's a shelf special and won't make the display frame. The funky little asymmetrical bird is pretty cool.

The needle tip Dalton is quartzite and has ground basal edges. The Dalton is definitely headed for the good frame, and dates to 7,000 years BP (before present).

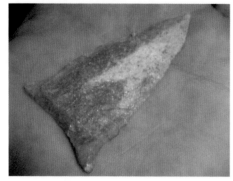

Close up of the quartzite Dalton.

Below is the point of the day, a knife made from green reeds spring chert-it's the one that was tombstoned.

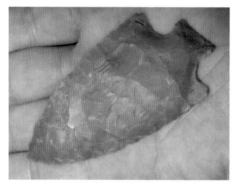

It was now about 4:15, and I was tired. I figure I was walking about 1/2 mile per hour, and covered about 2 miles zig-zagging the outer rim of Bass Islands. I paddled the mile and a half back, loaded up the yak, and drove home happy

Happy Hunting,
Willy B.

There are many ocean beach hunting locations. Ten thousand years ago glaciers trapped large amounts of fresh water. This meant ocean level was 200 feet below its current level. Many prehistoric Indian camps exist offshore under ocean waters. Venice beach in Florida has prehistoric campsites just out from the beach in 20 feet of water. McFadden Beach near Houston, Texas is probably the most well-known arrowhead producing ocean beach in North America. McFadden beach is famous for producing Paleo-Indian points 10,000 years old.

If you want to hunt ocean beaches be prepared to walk many miles. Points will be partly or fully exposed between the waterline and the sand dunes along the shore. Sometimes you can literally catch an arrowhead rolling in the surf. Greatly increase your odds of finding something good by hunting ocean beaches after major hurricanes. A giant storm leaves arrowheads strewn all up and down the beach if you look in the right places!

Gravel Bar Hunting

Gravel bar hunting takes place on creeks, rivers and lakes. Upstream Indian camps are eroding and depositing arrowheads into the river system. These points end up on river bottoms. Once exposed by low water levels, high spots on the river bottom become gravel bars.

Points aren't just on the top layer of gravel. When the water rises during flooding it turns the gravel over and brings new artifacts to light. Once you locate a gravel bar that produces (not all gravel bars produce artifacts) you can hunt it over and over again every time the river floods and recedes. Floods are the RESET button for gravel bars.

It is not necessary for there to be Indian camps anywhere near a particular gravel bar for it to produce arrowheads. However, the gravel bars immediately downstream from known artifact producing cut-banks often contain high concentrations of arrowheads. ALL gravel bars are worth giving the once over. You should search for flint flakes when hunting new gravel bars, as these are much more common than finished artifacts, and will be your first indicator that you need to slow down and search more carefully.

Searching for gravel bars is best accomplished from a canoe or kayak. Plan a day long float with friends and search every gravel bar (quick once over unless you find flakes, then slow walk it). Hunt very slowly and carefully on gravel bars below known campsites.

Some big rivers produce artifacts along their entire length for hundreds of miles. The Arkansas River in Oklahoma is famous for this. Arkansas River points have been polished by sand and are highly sought after by collectors. Every gravel bar on this river has produced artifacts. You can search gravel bars in downtown Tulsa and find really nice stuff to this day. The trick, once again, is being first after the floodwaters recede. These inner city gravel bars get heavy local pressure. Once after a flood, I went the very next day to the Arkansas River in downtown Tulsa and counted 15 people walking gravel bars, including 5 high school students wearing the same football jackets!

Large rivers like the Arkansas River are 1/4 mile wide and have HUGE gravel bars as far as the eye can see. This can

become psychologically overwhelming. I
focus on a small area in front of you and bloc
out. This allows hunting at night with headl
option. The small circle of light produced b
about all you can readily search at once
hunting is one way you can beat the heat, or beat the
competition if you time it right.

On big rivers, stay away from other people whenever
possible; you can get robbed at gunpoint out in the middle of
these rivers. It happens every year on urban sections of large
rivers. Your best bet is to avoid others by giving them plenty
of space. If you see someone moving towards you, move in
the same direction they are walking. This preserves the space
between you. I know several hunters who have been
confronted on gravel bars by armed, intoxicated landowners
on the Arkansas River in Oklahoma. DO NOT ARGUE with
landowners. Just move away as quickly as possible. High
winds make big river hunting next to impossible. Any gusts
over 20 mph turn the whole river into a giant sandblaster,
and it blasts your face and eyes. Avoid gravel bar hunting
during high winds.

Lakes have gravel bars on their bottom, usually covered by
deep silt. As lake levels drop, these gravel bars get washed
free of silt and become exposed in shallows. It is possible to
hunt gravel bars submerged in shallow receding water.
Unless the air is still, you will need an underwater viewer to
accomplish this. The slightest breeze will make ripples on the
water and you won't be able to see past the surface.

u are looking at the rocks, you are looking for the re of worked flint, as well as overall shape. Often the ar, base, tip, or even just an edge is all that shows. Look for these small PARTS of artifacts poking out.

Snorkeling

Snorkeling is great fun, and there is a lot to look at underwater, including plants and fish. Be sure to get a mask that is sized properly for you, leaks are annoying and will ruin your day. Learn the proper use of a snorkel and you will be able to keep your head under much longer and get way better results than with a mask alone. Fins are not necessary, as you should be moving slowly. Use your feet and walk along the bottom, facing into the waves or the current.

This Folding DIVER DOWN flag is being used from an anchored kayak on a lake. BELOW- Snorkeling on a 100 degree day summer 2012.

This technique is great for shallow clear water from 1 to 4 feet deep and should only be attempted below cut-banks known to produce artifacts, or lake sites submerged in shallow water. If you snorkel anywhere big enough for power boats, you are required by law to have a red diver down flag on a six foot pole. This flag warns others you are there under water and can keep you from being run over by power boats.

Be extra careful in creeks and rivers as fast moving water can pin you against sunken trees and other obstacles. Never snorkel alone. You need someone to watch you or at least snorkel with you. If you find something nice in the water, take it to shore or your boat immediately. I have found small arrowheads only to drop them accidentally and never recover them again. Secure your finds before continuing. I use a waterproof Pelican box with a foam insert. This Pelican box is essentially a portable arrowhead frame. Once I capsized after finding a really nice point, and lost the point when my kayak turned over. Since then I carry my floating waterproof portable frame everywhere when hunting. Snorkeling is a great beat the heat technique. You can employ this technique on river sites that get heavy pressure. Other hunters will hunt only where they can see to from the river bank, and points out deeper are yours for the taking.

If you want to get closer to the bottom in 5 to 10 feet of water you need a 30 pound lead weight belt with a quick release to keep you there. If you are kayaking this extra 30 pounds is a real pain to carry. You can bring a mesh bag and fill it with rocks. Put a 10 foot line on the bag with a foam water noodle on the other end of the rope. Drop the bag in 5 to 10 feet of water. Use the line to pull yourself to the bottom and hold onto the bag to stay down there for a minute or so. Anything that gets you closer to the bottom will greatly improve your results. Snorkeling is an exciting way to find artifacts, because water has a magnifying effect. Points look like HUGE SWORDS lying on the bottom. Expect them to shrink when you pick them up!

Scuba Diving

G9 GRAND recovered from a submerged site 10 feet deep.

DO NOT attempt this unless you are SCUBA certified. If you just buy some equipment and go for it, you could die, even in shallow water. This is the most risky type of arrowhead hunting, because you are 100% dependent on gear working properly. A sneeze can kill you SCUBA diving, literally.

I have successfully employed this technique in rivers and in lakes. The water in lakes is murky and you will only see the bottom in 10 feet of water or less.

You MUST use a DIVER DOWN flag on a six foot pole for your own safety. These red flags with a white slash across them can keep you from getting run over by a propeller. You will need a 30 pound lead weight belt with a quick release to keep you on the bottom.

SCUBA diving in fast moving rivers can kill you and is best avoided. You can safely SCUBA slow moving pools though. This technique is for known locations only. Submerged lake sites or pools below artifact producing cut-banks are usually lucrative. Even if you snorkel a pool, you can find more arrowheads in the same pool by SCUBA diving it. More time closer to the bottom will produce more artifacts.

It is possible to buy small "pony tanks" that have mouthpieces built into them and give you from 10 to 30 minutes of bottom time and are small enough to be kayak portable.

Death in 12 Feet of Water
May 2008

My buddy Larry from Florida has been hunting fossils and arrowheads since he was a child. Up until a few years ago it was legal to hunt artifacts on state owned rivers. Larry and his friend had been scuba diving together for a few years. The two of them had rescued MANY nice points that would have eventually been destroyed in the river.

They would take turns acting as spotters for each other just in case anything went wrong. Larry was on safety watch while his friend went under in 12 feet of water on a known site. About 20 minutes into the dive, Larry's friend came up waving his hands in distress, and immediately sunk back down. Larry jumped in and went after his buddy. Larry got him out, but it was too late.

Equipment was later tested and proved to be working perfectly. They were not diving deep enough to be on the dive charts, so nitrogen narcosis was eliminated as a contributing factor. It was theorized that the guy hiccupped or sneezed under water, which can cause water to be inhaled. No one knows for sure why the guy died, but he was only 27.

Larry brought some of his best finds to the funeral, and ritually "killed" them Indian-style by breaking them in half. The points were placed in the coffin.

Willy B.

SCUBA diving is the most dangerous way to hunt artifacts. Don't attempt this without SCUBA certification. Inexplicable deaths are not uncommon for divers. On the positive side, it PRODUCES RESULTS every time if you are diving known sites. It's creepy diving in murky lake water, you move along the bottom fanning with your hand. River pools are much clearer and easier to work in, but be careful in fast moving water.

The current can hold you against underwater objects and trap you down there! Think hard before trying this type of hunting. In a risk/reward analysis this would not be the best way to find arrowheads.

Spillway Hunting
Not for the Faint of Heart

Spillway hunting below hydroelectric dams is dangerous but very exciting. This is one of my favorite methods and NEVER fails to turn up arrowheads. Spillway hunting is very lucrative, requires no rain, and can be done any time the dam produces power. This is the most dangerous type of artifact hunting behind Scuba diving. Although you will cover more ground with a boat, you can do this type of hunting on foot. You can hunt gravel bars that are accessible by road. Spillway hunting is much safer on foot, but you won't find as much.

SPILLWAY MADNESS
Hunt Report, April 2012

So how bad do you REALLY want an arrowhead? I know where some are at, but we might get swept away by a flash flood if they open the dam.........

Yesterday the dam released water and the river went up to 16 feet for the first time in a LONG time, and then back down to 2 feet last night. I put the jet kayak in below the dam at noon and cruised DOWNSTREAM about 7 miles, then turned around and came back upstream, hunting the whole way. Usually I launch and go UPSTREAM first because this allows me to get back by floating downstream in case of mechanical failure. Today would be risky because they could open the spillway while I am below the dam, which can be very dangerous if you aren't ready for it. Once my boat FLOATED AWAY due to the floodgates being opened and rapid water rise! It was only luck that the boat snagged about 500 feet downstream- ALWAYS TIE UP YOUR BOAT if you walk away from it.

The first one turned out to be a beautiful round end scraper. The scraper had just washed out and had no chance to get damaged. I continued downstream to a known Indian campsite. In the picture below you can see the high water mark from last night.

An arrow point is barely visible in the bottom left corner.

Nice blue and white arrow point.

I found this large chert nodule split in half below one of my Indian camps. No doubt the Indians brought the nodule there, look how the points from today sort of disappear when you set them on it. These points were made from this same material.

This flint nodule matches the points!

I grubbed the Waubesa dart point from some slump mud. The broken drill came from a small feeder creek, it was fully exposed on a gravel bar.

I was headed back upstream and about 2,000 feet from the take out, the flood gates opened. The water rose quickly and the current was coming faster and faster. I was worried that I would not be able to make headway against it.

Lucky for me the oncoming current topped out around 13 mph. I was able to BARELY make headway, and inched my way against the broiling, swirling, rising current. It's a scary experience for the water to go from 2 feet to 16 feet in just a few minutes. It was an exciting end to a great hunt.

Willy B.

Use the United States Geological Survey real-time water data website to find water levels below hydroelectric dams. This type of hunting is exciting, but requires a lot of planning and local knowledge. Hydroelectric dams release water from their floodgates to produce power on demand. Most hydroelectric dams do not release continuously, they conserve water in their reservoirs and make power only during high demand situations, usually for daytime air conditioning demands in summer.

Consequently one local river below a power generating dam rises to 17 feet each day and goes back down to 4 feet every night. This 4 foot to 17 foot change is equal to a spring flood EVERY DAY. This means HUGE amounts of erosion compared to normal flow patterns. Basically 100 YEARS worth of spring flooding occurs every year on these sections of river. If you can find some riverbank Indian camps on these sections, you could hunt these camps every day and you will come up with new finds.

Obviously these rivers don't get hunted every day, and consequently MANY artifacts end up in the water. This allows for lucrative gravel bar hunting on the weekends when the water level is down low.

There is no set schedule for these water releases. Power producing dams are run by electric companies. You can call a phone number and get a recording that tells you what they PLAN to do for the next couple of days. But it's subject to change without notice.

All power producing dams have a warning siren, and if you are within a mile or two of the dam you will be able to hear the horn, and be forewarned of rapidly rising water. Usually, you won't hear anything because you are too far away, and that can be trouble. You need to remember to tie up your boat if you intend to walk away from it, or the rising water will take your boat away.

Most of the time the water is released on a regular schedule, and if you become familiar with it over time, it's less dangerous. The learning curve is steep in this type of hunting. Don't do this alone, especially in the beginning.

Warning: You Can Die Doing This Type of Hunting!
Safety rules for spillway hunting by boat:

In winter always pack a waterproof dry bag with a change of clothes in your boat. This can save your life if you fall in or capsize in cold weather. Always wear a lifejacket and keep it on all day. If you aren't wearing one, it can't save your life. Tell someone where you are going and when you will be back. Tie up your boat if you intend to walk away from it. Rising water can wash it downstream and leave you stranded.

Construction Site Hunting
FOLLOW THAT DUMPTRUCK!

When you hunt an active construction site you are truly rescuing arrowheads. Heavy machinery will destroy any artifacts in loose dirt on the site, unless you can get them first. Construction sites are a real boon to arrowhead hunters. Bulldozers and track-hoes often dig right through Indian camps when constructing roads and developing land. Check all open dirt. Any construction project near a creek or river is probably worth checking.

Permission

If you ask a construction site foreman for permission he will almost always say no. This is because he has insurance liability issues to worry about. Avoiding the foreman is the best choice. Your best chance is to ask a security guard after working hours.

If you see a security guard you can approach him and just ask if you can look in the open dirt for Indian arrowheads. If you don't see a security guard, start walking around and chances are one will find you. NEVER run from a security guard-you aren't doing anything wrong (unless you jumped a fence to get there-DO NOT JUMP FENCES). Tell him what you are doing. Honesty really is the best policy.

He will be relieved when you tell him you are looking for Indian arrowheads. If you offer to stay clear of construction materials and equipment the guard will often let you search the open dirt (he might tell you that if anyone else asks, he didn't give you permission!).

Road construction sites are usually in a public right of way and I have hunted many of them with impunity. There is no security guard and you just have to wait until everyone leaves after 5 pm or on weekends.

If you are finding good stuff on a construction site it's wise to pick up all the flint flakes you find and remove them. This will keep other hunters off your spot. Just like with any other method TIMING IS EVERYTHING. Fresh digging on a construction sites can produce artifacts, but for best results you need a good rain. Be the first one to hunt your spot after a good rain. Once I was able to get permission to dig an artifact rich construction site at night when no one was there. This was only because I knew the foreman, though. Construction site digging is artifact rescue. Artifacts are going to be destroyed as the construction digging continues, and even many years later when a building is eventually demolished.

Even small construction sites can pay off. I noticed a house being built near a local river. I saw a man there in a pickup truck and asked if he was the landowner. He was and I asked him if it would be okay for me to hunt arrowheads in the open dirt of his new house foundation. He was super friendly and agreed to let me hunt it no problem.

This turned out to be a really good spot and I was able to hunt it several times as the construction continued. I recovered 5 nice points from this small site

It took me 2 years to figure out arrowheads were being trucked off construction sites in wholesale quantity. Once you determine a construction site contains an Indian camp, you can follow the fill dirt. The dirt being removed contains artifacts. That dirt is going to be dumped out somewhere. FOLLOW THAT DUMPTRUCK! That's where the arrowheads are headed. I have pulled MANY points from dump truck piles, and you can hunt these piles EVERY TIME IT RAINS! Once I got on a dump truck pile so rich, I dug through it with my BARE HANDS and pulled out some good ones. A good dump truck pile can turn you into a human groundhog!

Wind Blown Sites
Any Old Desert Will Do........

Depending on where you live, a windstorm may be as effective at uncovering artifacts as a drenching rain. Sandy dry sites will be very good hunting after a blowout. High winds blow away the sand and dust exposing artifacts and it can be quite a bonanza if you get your timing right. Many blowouts leave artifacts fully exposed, like someone just set them down and walked away.

If you live in the desert southwest this may be the type of hunting for you, although anywhere that is flat and dry is especially good for blowout hunting. Sand dunes get moved around by high winds and can be lucrative areas to hunt as well. The west Texas desert is a well-known area for sandy open ground that produces artifacts after high winds-including the elusive and incredibly valuable FOLSOM point. During the dustbowl disaster of the 1930's there were many sites uncovered and large numbers of artifacts were found. The recent heat waves and drought conditions can produce just the right conditions for blowout hunting.

GO GLOBAL WARMING!

High Mountain Campsites

Although creeks and rivers were in fact the highways of ancient Indians, you do not have to be in or near a creek or river to find points. Indians traveled across land also, and even camped high up mountains far from water sources. In the winter you could melt the abundant snow to obtain water, and you would not necessarily need to have a spring, creek, or river there to meet your needs. If you find a campsite in high mountains note the elevation, other campsites will tend to be at these same elevations throughout the mountains of the area. I suspect these high mountain sites were temporary hunting camps, but no one knows for sure.

Many archaic campsites are located on mountain tops, with very little protection from the wind. These campsites are often found on the first or second terrace down from the top of the mountain. I have found nice points on mountain tops with really nice views, but most of these were isolated finds. I think the Indians might have climbed some mountains to get a good view, like we do today.

In archaeologists have been hunting snow patches in Canada and Alaska on high-altitude mountain sites using helicopters. Global warming is melting snow patches that have remained frozen year round for 10,000 years. These snow patches are spots in mountain shadow at high altitude. When winter snow melts away during summer sun, these shaded patches remain covered with snow several feet deep all summer long. Game animals are attracted to these snow patches in summer to get water. Game animals attracted ancient hunters. Many darts and spears were lost in these snow patches when Indians missed their mark. Some were never recovered. These melting patches reveal bone and stone projectile points often still mounted in their original shafts! The organic bone points and wooden projectile shafts have been preserved from decay by the cold. Arrowhead hunting by helicopter with the chance of finding ultra-rare organic artifacts; sign me up! It's probably the ONLY time I have been jealous of archaeologists. Most archaeologists don't do much surface hunting, they only do field work a couple weeks a year, and usually it involves digging.

Pinch Points and Isolated Finds

An isolated find is an arrowhead found in a random spot without the usual flint flakes and camp rock indicators. Sometimes arrowheads are found in places where there could not possibly be a camp, and for no apparent reason. Indian camps are great because artifacts are concentrated there. However, that does not mean you won't find artifacts in other places. Arrowheads can turn up anywhere.

Indians stashed stone tools for many reasons, and usually this meant burying them under or near some landmark for future retrieval. Many times these stashes were never recovered. If you find 2 or more stone tools stacked together, it is considered a "cache" (pronounced cash).

Animals and people will travel the path of least resistance, as dictated by features in the terrain. Pinch points are funnel areas game animals are forced through by natural obstacles. A good deer hunter knows where these places are, and sets up his tree stand at these pinch points. These are great places to sit and wait for game to come to you. Steep riverbanks, bluffs, hills, mountains, giant boulders, and lake shores are all examples of terrain features that force animals to travel certain paths.

Isolated find July 2010 near a public fishing access.

G10 Dickson made from Jefferson City chert-it's a SMOKER! This is one of the finest points in my collection.

Just like people today drop and misplace things, so did the Indians of prehistory. Some arrows missed their mark, and were lost in vegetation or snow, never to be recovered. While the shafts are long ago weathered away, the arrowheads are still there, even thousands of years later. I suspect Indian "pockets" were not all that great, and many stone tools were simply dropped. There were no safety deposit boxes for ancient man to store his valuables.

Locating pinch points can be as simple as locating a low water crossing. Animals are forced to seek out these low water crossings to avoid deep water or swift currents. Indians made use of these pinch points when hunting animals just like hunters do today. These natural game funnels are in the same locations they were thousands of years ago. I have located many artifacts at low water crossings and pinch points. You won't find flint flakes or camp rocks at these places, just projectile points.

Using Techniques in Combination
Check Everything, Not Just Your X's

Combining surface hunting techniques is like a boxer using combination punches. You will be MUCH more effective, and have a better chance of KNOCKING SOME ARTIFACTS OUT! If you follow the water hunting techniques in this book, you will plan 6 mile float trips and draw your own map marked with X's where you suspect Indian camps might be located. Then when you float the route, you will check the riverbank in these marked locations for flint flakes, camp rocks, and arrowheads.

When you find camp site indicators, you can then snorkel the water below these cut-banks or use your underwater viewer. You can grub the slump mud below these banks with your bare hands. Pay special attention to the gravel bars immediately downstream from river banks that produce flint flakes and artifacts. These gravel bars have arrowheads on them. If you find a creek right next to a bank that produces arrowheads, walk up the creek a little ways and look for points in the water. Hunt every gravel bar you find exposed during your float with a quick once-over, then much slower if you find a flake or point. All gravel bars are worth a once-over.

Combining ALL applicable techniques in a hunt will greatly increase your production. Slow down. Be deliberate. In the river moving fast works against your personal safety, and you miss artifacts if you go too fast!

Chapter 8: Scheduling Your Hunts

Windows of Opportunity

Windows of opportunity appear when Indian artifacts are uncovered by rain, floods, farm machinery, construction, or wildlife. Imagine an open window in a wooden frame magically appearing in mid-air every time an artifact becomes exposed. If you get your timing right, you can reach right through the open window and pick up an arrowhead.

Rain is a surface hunter's friend. Rain erodes campsites and washes out arrowheads with every storm. Enough rain to flood a river is even better. Windows of opportunity appear right after these erosional events. A freshly plowed field by the river might have 30 open windows floating over it after a 3 inch rain. Windows are nowhere, then suddenly everywhere, and they tend to appear in the same places over and over.

However, rain is not the only game in town. Wave action uncovers an arrowhead, and a window appears on the lake shore. Hydroelectric dams create a spring flood every day, and windows appear down the banks of the river. A construction machine digs right through an Indian camp, and windows suddenly appear. A gopher spits an artifact out of its hole, and a window appears in the middle of the woods.

How long will the windows remain? These windows will disappear as soon as the artifact is picked up by another hunter, plowed under by the tractor, washed away by the river, or paved over by machinery. Windows do not hang around long.

Your mission is to figure out where and when these windows will appear, and be there to reach through and pick up your arrowheads. You will accomplish this through information management, technology, Sherlock Holmes level detective work, and if necessary, voodoo magic. Expert arrowhead hunters are not screwing around.

The Process

I find my advantage through information management and technology. I call these advantages force multipliers because they allow me to find as many artifacts as a small army. For me it's ALMOST as much fun planning a hunt as actually hunting. I do my most important work BEFORE I leave the house. A good plan will produce artifacts EVERY TIME. Where erosion and campsite locations intersect, there will be arrowheads. In the final step, I consider when other hunters might be hunting so I can get there before them.

———————————————————

HUNT REPORT December 2012

Arctic Camo Surprise

Night before last there were spotty thunderstorms across half the state.

RAIN-lovely, lovely RAIN. Life for me is good with a little rain, and even better with a whole lot.   It's practically a ritual for me to be lost in some sort of map of one type or another. Correlating weather with known Indian camp locations is almost as much fun as actually hunting artifacts. It's like winning when your spots get nailed by a downpour-especially if life doesn't get in the way and you are fortunate enough to have the very next morning free to go look. Being first on known camps almost guarantees a find in some locations.

We use code names for Indian camps so we can discuss them without giving away locations. Artifact collections are really great, but my most prized possession is my collection of campsite locations. By correlating my site list with a rain map I came up with four good options.

1. An awesome field I call the" field of dreams" just got hit with an inch of rain. I called the landowner and he just planted winter wheat 2 days ago-it's still germinating in the field. Scratch that.

2. A decent lake site I named bird-shit island, because it was so white with gull crap the first time I was there it looked covered in snow from a distance! The lake got so low the island turned into a peninsula, and the entire peninsula (2 acres or so) is covered with flint, camp rocks, arrowheads, and silt. Each time it rains a little silt washes away, exposing new stuff.

Bird-shit island got hit with 3/4 of an inch of rain. The only problem here is access-no ordinary bass boat or john boat can get there because the water is only 12 inches deep for about a mile approaching this site. Hunting this site requires kayaking several miles and then back out again.

The shallow water is a two edged sword; it keeps other people from getting there but it's a long paddle in dead calm water.

3.   Another lake site on a different lake called Ian's landing consists of several banks along the lake shore. Ian's landing got hit with 2 inches of rain in a relatively short time and there is probably a point just lying there, freshly washed out. The negative here is an 80 mile drive one way. Not off the list, but closer would be a lot better.

Anything within 100 miles is worth consideration, but if I keep it under 50 miles one-way it allows me more hunts for the same weekly gas expense.

4.   This lake site is on a 3rd lake in a completely different direction. This is my newest site found only 3 days ago. I call it C & H (as in pure cane sugar-named for the sugar quartz point I found there) and it got hit with 2 inches of rain. C & H consists of about 1000 feet of high bank with a 30 foot relatively steep exposure between the bank and the water's edge.   With normal water levels this bank is completely underwater. It's 100% sand and looks like a beach covered with flint flakes, camp rocks, and arrowheads.

This spot had been extensively hunted by locals as evidence by zigzag footprints on my previous hunt.   But C & H has that "magic angle" that erodes itself when rained on (silt covered lake sites like bird shit island are too level for this killer type of erosion). Plus this was within my preferred 50 mile limit.

By the numbers, we have a clear winner: C & H. This is in spite of the fact I hunted it only 3 days earlier. After 2 inches of rain, there are points sitting there right now. Can I get there before the windows close?

I hit the highway and pulled onto a gravel road for the last mile before the lake. The last time I was here (only 3 days ago when I had first discovered the site) I was able to get within 20 feet of the lake shore. Experience told me that would not be the case with 2 inches of fresh rain. I would need to be very careful on this last part as getting stuck in the mud would be likely.

There was only one impassible puddle between me and the top of the last sand hill at the lake edge. You can't just drive through these, even if you recently navigated them when dry. There can be deep holes and sometimes you won't come out the other side.   I jumped out, put on my knee high rubber boots and grabbed a probe. Then I walked through the 12' x 12' puddle, probing for deep holes as I went along.

I located a feasible track with about a foot of water at its deepest part. That's pretty much over my limit in a front wheel drive minivan. But if you get a good run at it, inertia will usually get you through to the other side. Usually. I backed up, took a run, and "ka-doosh" a giant splash and mess. But I came out the other side, wheels turned and spinning.

I had to park on the top of the last sand hill and would be dragging my kayak 100 feet down to the water's edge. No problem dragging a 38 pound kayak DOWN this embankment. But, coming back up would not be fun. Dragging back up won't be necessary though. I have 100 feet *of poly rope I tie to my trailer hitch and I will use the van to pull the loaded kayak (hopefully weighed down with pointy rocks!) up the embankment.*

I geared up, pulled out the kayak, and took the downhill AT A RUN pulling the kayak. Guess I was pretty excited. It's about one mile to the right and across the lake to C & H.

It was 9:05 am, 50 degrees, overcast, and in spite of a predicted 5-8 mph wind (tolerable) it was dead calm. A mile's paddle and a channel crossing later I was on C & H.

Upon a closer inspection I noticed that all signs of footprints that had been there only 3 days ago had been completely obliterated by the rain. The entire beach exposure was smooth from cut-bank to water with no tracks of other hunters present.

The windows were open, now all I have to do is reach through...........

I spent a total of 5 hours meticulously hunting C & H. I flipped hundreds of flint flakes. Came up with broken points right away, and kept finding them. About 3 hours in I discovered an older transitional paleo point, but it was missing its tip. There were awesome serrations on this point, and it was inches from the water line. Minutes later, I found another serrated older blade about 10 feet away (both these older points could have been made by the same person, with diamond shaped cross sections from steep re-sharpening). The second one was tip dinged and base broke, but made from reeds spring chert.

I was pretty happy with 2 transitional-paleo brokes, but still wanted a whole point and kept looking very carefully. Then, an edge poked out of the sand and it looked like maybe an ear.........

Pulled out this little Reeds Spring chert corner notch projectile point-in a rare variety that resembles arctic camo. Pictured below are some of the days finds. The blue point in the upper left looks great-until you turn it over.....

The mother of all flint stacks on its back side!

This is a complete artifact, sharp all the way around with a good tip, and relatively thin but for the flint stack on its face. The maker was probably one very aggravated Indian to get this far into a piece and not be able to clean up this rough spot in his rock. This piece would still be perfectly useable as a knife, it's sharp and thin all the way around.

Two transitional paleo brokes, and an arctic camo surprise.

C & H lived up to its name and produced a small sugar quartz rice shallow side notch resharpened to the nub, but still a looker. (Bottom right hand in photo above.) Extracted myself and my gear, and went home very happy to squeak out this blue, grey, and white arctic camo point. Covered most of the spectrum today--birdies, rice side notch, Dickson, and a couple older points-definitely a multi-component site with woodland, archaic, and trasitional-paleo occupations present.

Happy Hunting,
Willy B

Correlating Weather and Campsite Locations

You will need access to a computer for hunt planning and preparation. If you don't have access to the internet, GET IT. A computer is the single most important piece of equipment for planning a hunt.

The National Weather Service is the best source of information for rainfall amounts and storm radar. Watch where the storm goes and then check rainfall totals and river levels. You can do this from your computer any time of day.

Most weather websites use the government's data to produce their maps and charts. Do yourself a favor and bypass these second hand information merchants. Use government websites directly and there will be no advertisements getting in the way and slowing down your map loading.

The National Weather Service Storm Totals Precipitation Maps are the key to your surface hunting after rainstorms. The total amount of rainfall for any given storm is shown on a color coded map of your state. With this map alone you can determine how much rain has fallen on any given Indian campsite you have previously located.

It's also good to keep in mind that if it rains 3 inches in an hour, that creates much more erosion than if it rains 3 inches in a day. A short duration heavy rainfall works in your favor every time.

SCHEDULING RIVER HUNTING

Follow the Flood

To check the water level of any river or creek use the United States Geological Survey (USGS) real time surface water data web page. This government funded system uses remote sensors in every river in your state for REAL TIME water level measurements.

Rivers will flood after a good rain. Any Indian campsites you have found on a river bank will be heavily eroded during river floods. When the water goes back down, flint flakes, camp rocks, and arrowheads will be left, some fully exposed, for you to pick up. Your mission is to watch these water levels, and be the first one there when the levels comes back down. You will find arrowheads using this method.

SCHEDULING LAKE HUNTS

Follow the Drought

You can find lake levels on many fishing websites, along with water temperature information. Lakes are a little more complicated because you need to keep track of these levels over time. It's not enough to know the level of a lake on any given day, you need to know what the level was the day before so you can tell if it drops or rises. You should hunt when water levels go down. Dropping water levels during times of drought expose submerged Indian Camps.

SEASONAL CONSIDERATIONS

Many arrowhead hunters only hunt in the spring when it rains on freshly plowed fields, and they will tell you it's the only time of year worth looking for arrowheads. Rain and plowing are advantageous to arrowhead hunters, but are not limiting factors. Artifacts can be found REGARDLESS of season, precipitation, or agricultural plowing schedules.

Arrowhead hunting is a year round hobby for most of the lower 48 states. With knowledge and proper gear THERE ARE NO LIMITS to when you can successfully find arrowheads-(see Chapter 13: When there is No Rain).

WINTER

Winter is the best time for artifact hunting. No bugs, no heat, no poison ivy, no COMPETITION, and lower than normal water levels combine to make it a great time of year to find an arrowhead. Snow is the ONLY limiting factor I have encountered-and as long as your local rivers aren't completely frozen over and covered with snow, you can STILL find arrowheads on gravel bars and in the water!

Winter river hunting introduces a new variable that actually creates MORE bank slump than flooding. It's called the freeze/thaw cycle, and you will learn to love it. On winter nights many times it goes below 32 degrees, and freezes cut-banks which remain wet from soaking up river water through wicking action. When the sun comes up in the morning, temperatures start to rise above freezing.

This temperature rise causes thermal expansion, and pushes large chunks of bank into the river. The bulk of erosion actually occurs in the winter, not from rain flooding.

Frozen rivers are also good for business (the business of finding points). When temperatures rise and the river ice starts to break up, large chunks of ice sometimes hundreds of feet long, act as plows, and plow up gravel bars, turning over rocks and releasing once hidden artifacts.

Dickson under 1" thick ice. I had to use a rock to break the ice. In the winter vegetation is dead and leaves are down, allowing you a better view of the countryside. You can spot features which may be invisible at other times of the year, and gain access to spots that you could not get to when poison ivy covered every inch of river banks.

Weather Can Kill You

Lightning is deadly. Hail can definitely kill you. High winds can kill you in many ways, including by dropping large "widow maker" branches on your head. Once I was walking along a river bank and 15 feet in front of me a large branch from a dead tree fell and stuck straight into the ground like a spear.

Part of planning any hunt is checking the forecast for the day. The best plan in the world won't make any difference if you find yourself in the middle of a thunderstorm or high winds.

High winds make canoeing or kayaking difficult. The working limit for kayaking is about 15 mph sustained wind. Anything over that, you should wait for a different and less windy day. 20 mph wind gusts make chop on open water, this chop will spit water into your face if you are boating, impairing your vision and making you miserable, even in a power boat.

You may find yourself unable to make forward progress in a canoe or kayak with any wind speed over 15 mph. High winds can actually reverse surface current in sections of a river, and suddenly your downstream float becomes an upstream slog.

Unintended Consequences
October 2011

A Cautionary Tale

This fellow I know wanted to go arrowhead hunting. I agreed to take him to a good lake site that produces arrowheads. We took my kayaks and drove 40 miles to the spot. We found some brokes and one nice corner notch dart point. He noticed the lake was low at the time, and I told him that was why we were there. Low lake levels expose ancient campsites. I told him the same thing I tell everyone when I show them a hunting spot, "Come here anytime you want, but I would appreciate a call so I don't waste my own time driving all the way here to find someone else already cleaned it out." I figure that's a reasonable request after having showed somebody a good arrowhead hunting spot.

Unbeknownst to me, this fellow showed my spot to his buddy Jason. I knew Jason and had dug arrowheads with him, but he was not in my immediate circle of friends. The following spring, rains flooded the lake to record levels. Drought conditions came by October and the lake came all the way back down to expose these same camps.

I was watching the water level on the computer, and knew the EXACT day when those camps were going to be exposed. I was doing my preliminary work planning to go hunt the spot. Due diligence required me to check the weather, and when I saw sustained winds of 25 mph, the hunt was cancelled and put off until winds would be down to a safe speed.

Jason, working on his own, realized the water would be down that next day. Jason was a real go-getter, but had little experience surface hunting. He decided to go on his own, taking his brother's canoe and two of his buddies. The three guys went to the boat ramp, put the canoe in, and went across a small cove to the first camp. They had not even crossed the main channel. They pulled their canoe up to the shore, got out, and started hunting artifacts.

At some point not long after their arrival on the camp, Jason's canoe was blown from the shoreline into the lake. By the time they noticed, it was 20 feet out in the lake and gaining speed. Jason did not have his lifejacket on, it was in the canoe. He did not want to lose his brother's canoe, so he jumped in the water fully clothed with his shoes on, swimming after the canoe. The two with him said he made 2 or 3 swimming strokes, went under, and was never seen again.

They dredged his body up 2 days later. He was 23, and newly married to a pregnant wife. Everyone said he was a good swimmer, but that doesn't make much difference if you have your clothes and shoes on with no life jacket.

I got a phone call the day after Jason drowned, from the guy who had shown Jason the spot. He explained what happened and that Jason was dead.

There are three lessons to be learned here.

Lesson number 1: Don't show anyone your spot unless you want the whole world to know about it. The guy you show takes another guy, and that person takes someone else. It quickly becomes a cascade of people and you end up with no artifacts from that spot again. This has happened to me before, but never included DEATH as a consequence!

Lesson number 2: ALWAYS wear your life jacket, even when you are out of the boat. My guess is Jason was not a knowledgeable or experienced canoeist. NOBODY should canoe without wearing a life preserver, no matter what their experience level. Just having the life jacket with you is not good enough.

Lesson number 3: Avoid sustained winds of 15 mph and over when canoeing or kayaking. High winds make waves that can overtop and sink a boat. Your boat can be blown from the shoreline, leaving you stranded. ALWAYS tie up your boat or pull it onto the shore.

I don't know which situation is worse; a new guy who won't wear his life preserver, or an experienced person who refuses to wear one. ALWAYS WEAR YOUR LIFE JACKET when floating on open water, and KEEP IT ON ALL DAY. If you don't care about your own life, the water will take it from you.

We have changed the nickname of this spot to THE DROWNING POOL. I have been back there many times since Jason drowned. I have found some pretty nice points too. The strange thing is that the cove where he drowned is VERY shallow, and there are only a couple of deep holes there. He had been swimming right over one when he drowned. ALWAYS wear your lifejacket when boating. If it's not on you, it can't save your life. Avoid sustained winds of 15 mph or more.

Willy B.

High summer temperatures are life threatening. When temperatures get above 90 degrees, you need to plan carefully. Plenty of water is a no brainer. To hunt safely in temperatures of 90 degrees or more, you need to use methods that allow you to be IN THE WATER all day. Keeping parts of your body in the water is essential on days like these, especially if its 100 degrees or more.

Even walking ankle deep in a spring fed creek will suffice. The water acts like a heat sink and radiator, and cools your blood as it flows through your feet and returns through your heart and brain. These are also good days for snorkeling points from the river bottom.

Always put safety first. What good is finding arrowheads if you aren't around to enjoy having found them?

When Should You Leave the House?

In order to optimize the useable hours in a day, it is necessary to adjust the time you leave the house based on the time of year. My goal is to hunt year round, but maintain certain comfort standards. If you are organized, this is not a problem.

My summer schedule is based on beating the heat. Most of my hunts are day trips, and in the heat of the summer earlier is better. I often leave my house a full hour before sunrise. This allows me travel time to my destination, and I can launch my boat or start my hike AT SUNRISE. The morning hours are much more comfortable, and it doesn't start being REALLY uncomfortable or dangerous until around 11 am. That usually gives me 6 full hours to pull one out.

Winter hunting schedule has to do with wind and temperature. In the winter you have to consider wind chill. Even a 5 mph sustained wind can make the "feels like" temperature 10 degrees lower than actual ambient temperature. To beat the cold I don't leave the house until 10 am. This puts me at the parking area by 11 am and temperatures are MUCH more comfortable than in the early morning. It gets dark by 5 pm in the winter, and that means up to 6 useable hours, during which the temperature rises.

Minimum requirements for a COMFORTABLE and safe winter hunt are 40 degrees with FULL sun and wind gusts of 5 mph or less (preferably no wind!). You can hunt when its 35 degrees and wind gusts up to 15 mph, but that's the working limit, colder than that you will be miserable.

Learning to Love Maps
Habitual Ritual

Topographic maps looks pretty confusing at first, but it's worth learning how to read them. Maps will save you many hours of aimlessly wandering around looking down. It is pre-hunt ritual to have my head buried in one sort of map or another.

Topographic maps are essentially contour maps, and they allow you to see 3 dimensional shapes of the land by reading lines drawn in only 2 dimensions on a flat page or screen.

Much has been written on the subject of interpreting topographic maps. Unfortunately most of these writings read like Department of Motor Vehicle study guides, and don't really explain what is relevant.

In a Nut Shell.......

Color of lines and areas on these maps are very important. Contours of land are represented by brown lines for contours above water, and blue lines for contours under water. Each contour is a line of equal elevation; contour lines NEVER CROSS-they are concentric.

Concentric: of or denoting circles or other shapes that share the same center, with the larger completely surrounding the smaller. In effect each mountain is represented by a bullseye configuration of lines that never cross, but instead of being circular represent the outline of the mountain. The small center of this bullseye represents the top of the mountain and the largest ring represents the base of that mountain. Each ring on the bullseye represents a 20 foot change in elevation. The closer these rings are spaced, the steeper the terrain. The more space between the rings in the bullseye, the more gradual the slope.

To help the map reader determine elevation, INDEX CONTOURS are placed at every fifth line, and are wider and colored darker brown, with elevation numbers spaced along them. Elevation numbers are height above sea level expressed in feet.

Black lines represent highways and roads.

Blue lines indicate creeks and rivers.

Water is marked in blocks of light blue.

Forest is indicated by blocks of light green.

Heavily urbanized areas are depicted by blocks of pink.

Various symbols are used to depict features such as buildings, campgrounds, springs, water tanks, mines, and caves. These symbols can be found in the map key, usually at the bottom of topo maps.

Paper Maps   vs.   Electronic Maps

I recommend paper maps even if you choose to carry a handheld GPS unit. It can get tedious and confusing trying to view small handheld GPS screens, and paper maps are much easier to use. You can get paper USGS topographic maps from the United States Geological Survey website (7 dollars each at the time of this writing). For purposes of artifact hunting, you will need to order maps scaled at 1: 24,000 and each map of this scale represents about 7 square miles. In the long run, these maps are more expensive than a handheld GPS, but they sure are NICE and a heck of a lot easier to use.

You do not have to buy paper topographic maps. They can be viewed free online and printed out in small sections. Google Maps is a free online service (you have to download the topographic overlay for Google maps), and there are several good commercial map sites available for a fee. I like to use Acme Mapper which is free and provides an easy way to toggle between topographic maps, road maps, and satellite photos. If you want to print out a map, get the section you want on your computer screen, and do a "screen dump" to your printer. This is accomplished by holding down the control key and pressing the "p" key once.

Modern technology allows you to carry a waterproof handheld GPS in the field. Handheld waterproof GPS units cost less money compared to buying a bunch of USGS paper maps. The weakness of GPS units is battery life. Make sure batteries are fully charged before leaving on your hunt.

Even if you buy a GPS, it's best to study online topo maps before you leave, and draw your own small "patrol maps" indicating roads, rivers, creeks, and major landmarks in the area. Mark your X's indicating your predicted Indian camp locations on your patrol map, and enter them as waypoints on your GPS. Drawing patrol maps is part of every hunt for me. Patrol maps give me backup in case I break my GPS or run out of batteries. Technology can break down. Play it safe and draw your own maps anyway. It's a bad feeling to be lost in the woods. Drawing your own patrol maps is a method of studying the area you are going into. Even if you lose your GPS and your paper map, you will still be able to remember some basic knowledge of the area.

The bones of a successful hunt are created before you leave the house, and fleshed out later in the field. Do your homework, and you will be rewarded with arrowheads.

Chapter 9: Successful Mindset & Winning Strategies

Setting the Stage for Your Success

"I'm going to give you a little advice. There's a force in the universe that makes things happen. All you have to do is get in touch with it, stop thinking, and let things happen."

--Ty Webb

If you want to be the best at anything, you must create a winning mindset and reality. Thoughts and attitude manifest physical results. You have to believe in yourself.

Expert artifact hunters have resolve and confidence; we do whatever it takes to get the job done. We are not screwing around. If you want to hunt artifacts on an elite level, you need an elite frame of mind. If the playing field was a teeter totter, an elite hunter is the 800 pound gorilla and it would take 6 ordinary men on the other side to level it out.

Timing Is Everything

The 3 most important rules of arrowhead hunting : Be First. Be First. Be First.

If these 3 rules were all you knew, you could bypass this entire book and you would still be successful. Even if you only hunt a single campsite that gets heavy hunting pressure, be first after a big rain and you will find arrowheads. Get up at 5am, and be there at dawn. If someone else is there when you get there, come at 3 am next time and hunt with a headlamp.

You are not the only artifact hunter out there. If it rains on your best Indian campsite Wednesday, and you wait until the weekend to go hunt it, your odds of finding something REALLY good are greatly reduced. If life doesn't get in your way, hunt IMMEDIATELY after a good rain.

Collect Sites, Not Points

This sounds simple, but it's not. You need to know camp locations in the first place to take full advantage of timing. Anytime I can find a new site for my site list, even if it's got footprints on every square inch, that's a WIN. A day without a whole point but with a new site for my site list is a WIN. Finding campsites is a win because an expert KNOWS the day will come when weather conditions and campsite locations intersect. Then he will be the first one there, and he will find arrowheads.

Success and failure have different definitions once you adopt this mindset. This way of thinking puts you squarely in the game for the long haul, and eliminates a lot of the frustration beginners have when they hike all day and come up with no artifacts. Short term thinking (collecting points) is setting yourself up for failure. If finding arrowheads was easy, everyone would be doing it. In the beginning there will be MANY days you will come home with no arrowheads. Collecting campsite locations creates a frame of mind where a day with no good finds can still be considered a successful day!

Most artifact hunters collect arrowheads. Expert arrowhead hunters collect Indian campsite locations. Arrowheads are just an effect, campsites are the cause. These campsite locations represent the true value of your collection. Your site list is your most valuable possession. If you sell all your rocks, it wouldn't matter as long as you have your site list. A good site list is your ticket to an endless supply of arrowheads!

Plan B- The No Skunk Zone

While I do appreciate my broken points, and each is fascinating in its own way, an expert hunter with a large site list finds complete points every time he hunts. A complete point might not be perfect, but it will have no damage and will be as it was originally made. Finding artifacts costs money and time, and getting skunked (coming home empty handed) is not on the agenda of an expert artifact hunter.

This means you will always have Plan B. Plan B is ANOTHER campsite, usually a short drive from Plan A, just in case your first plan doesn't produce. This makes the difference between getting skunked and bringing home the goods from the woods (arrowheads!).

Choose your Plan B carefully. If you are hunting after a rain, choose your Plan A and B based on where the most rainfall occurred. Plan B does not have to be located RIGHT NEXT to Plan A, it just needs to be in the same general direction.

When there is no rain, your options include locating man-made erosion, construction sites, or digging. You build the framework for a successful artifact hunt BEFORE you leave the house.

Once you correlate your site list with erosion (or lack of erosion) you make a list of viable hunting options. Plan A will be your best option based on man-made or natural erosion on known campsites, and your ability to BE FIRST on any given location after an erosional event. Knowing campsite locations, timing your hunt, and knowledge of your competition all play a part in successfully recovering artifacts.

If Plan A produces something really good, finish Plan A, and go home. Mission accomplished. If you follow your original plan and fail to produce a complete point, then it's time for Plan B. Plan B can turn an otherwise average day into a great one. For beginners, Plan B can even be a new spot you have never been before, but looks good on the map.

Exploring
Grow or Die

You need to go new places you have never set foot before, or you will not find enough sites to keep this circus in business. Remember that discovering new Indian campsite locations is just as important as good timing for a beginner. You need to know WHERE before being overly concerned with WHEN.

When you are new you should spend 50% of you time exploring new places you have never been. This is essential to building your site list. Once you get over 50 sites, you can rest on your laurels to a great degree. With 50 sites on your list, exploring becomes less important. I have 77 personal found Indian camps within 100 miles of my house as of the time of this writing, and many of them encompass 3 or 4 nearby occupations at each location.

Once you get that many camps your problem is choosing which one to hunt on any given day. While you might get to hunt more than one, you will probably be FIRST on one site only, especially after a good rain. Choose well. I pick camps that produce better quality and size over camps that produce large numbers of field grade points.

This is the problem you want to have: which camp do I hunt first?   Once you have that problem, you are an expert arrowhead hunter.

Controlling Your Information
Knowledge is Power

When you find a REALLY good site tell no one. This is the most difficult part, really. You must learn to STFU. Telling anyone your site locations can have SERIOUS repercussions you may have never considered.

Don't Tell Joe-Tale of the Clovis Spot
May 2011

The best spot in town has been compromised for everyone. It all starts innocently enough.

You show Joe at work your Clovis point, and he thinks it's really cool. Next thing you know you have agreed to take Joe hunting at your spot. You and Joe go there, and Joe finds a G9 Afton that's as thin as a credit card (never fails) while you get skunked.You make Joe promise to not tell anyone else or bring anyone else there, because it's really not even your spot-your other buddy showed it to you, and made YOU promise.............

TWO WEEKS LATER

After a 2 inch rain, you and the ORIGINAL SITE FINDER go to the Clovis spot only to find another co-worker (who Joe told) and 4 other people who came with him.

Turns out they have permission, but only for this one time. The landowner told them too many people were coming around asking, and after that day NO ONE would be allowed back in.

OOPS- Serious consequences if you tell JOE.
DON'T TELL JOE. Tell Joe = No Arrowhead.

Willy B.

Be careful who you trust, this is not a casual enterprise. You will cause yourself pain and anguish if you can't learn to keep your secrets. You will find artifacts where windows of opportunity and finite resources intersect. Telling others when and where you are going is a VERY BAD IDEA. Choose your hunting partners wisely.

Hunting Partners

Take this subject lightly at your own peril. You NEED a hunting partner to accomplish most of these missions safely. I would rather hunt with a partner every time if possible. A hunting partner can go for help if you get hurt and have no cell phone signal. A hunting partner can be there to share the joy of an awesome find. A hunting partner can drive a second car for your kayak shuttle.

Most people make TERRIBLE arrowhead hunting partners. It comes down to greed. Surface hunting with another person means splitting what's there to be found, and it's never a fair split. Most people who find something good while hunting with you will not even consider that you might be a little upset at having found nothing yourself. A lousy hunting partner keeps right on chugging after a good find and says stuff like "I guess that point was just meant for me. Hyuk, hyuk, hyuk." A good arrowhead hunting partner is someone who finds a killer, then hangs back and lets you take the lead, so you get a fair shot.

Let me tell you, this is a RARE, RARE trait in any person. It happens to be my default response when I find a smoker. I hold back and let my buddy have a shot. This also extends to site knowledge. I know where all the hotspots are on each of my sites. If I just found a killer, I might say "go over there and hunt that dark area by the trees". Thereby directing my hunting partner to an area I know has a greater probability of producing a nice point.

One of my early mentors refuses to hunt with experienced hunting partners. He only takes new people who have no idea where or how to look for arrowheads. He calls them VICTIMS. A victim is a person who splits the gas cost and calls 911 if you fall off a bluff; but he doesn't end up with any of the nice arrowheads. A victim is just there to watch you find arrowheads, but he doesn't know it. Purposely hunting with victims is bad karma, you will get better results in the end hunting with an equal. A friend you can trust is worth a hundred G-10 artifacts.

I "interviewed" 14 people before finding 2 good candidates for the "job" of arrowhead hunting partner. It's amazing how many people will apply for a "job" that only pays arrowheads!

I recently lost a 3rd longtime hunting partner when I found him in one of my best camps after a big rain. My policy is if I show you one of my good camps, you can go there without me, but you need to tell me you are going there so I don't waste my time hunting a spot you just cleaned out. I consider this a reasonable request after showing someone my camp location in the first place.

I spotted his truck at the river access one morning. I was pretty angry and set out down the river in my jet kayak. If he would have called me we could have hunted it together. People who don't call are being greedy, they want ALL the arrowheads for themselves, and they are too lazy to find their own spots. People who do this have no self-respect, and no respect for anyone else.

He was gone when I arrived at the field. Later I found out he had walked downriver on foot, and had heard me coming. He knew no other boat could even run in water that shallow. He knew I was coming and I would not be happy. So he hid from me, and ran back to his truck. I hunted in his footprints and came up with a couple brokes. His truck was gone when I returned. I still had plan B, so it worked out fine for me.

Trust is like a beautiful flower; once it's crushed it will never be the same again. We won't be hunting together again, and if I see him on one of my camps, I don't know how I will react, but I can't imagine it would be positive.

Harvesting Your Arrowheads

Expert arrowhead hunters HARVEST ARROWHEADS, they don't really hunt for them. I look at it like planting a crop. A farmer invests a lot of time plowing the ground, planting seeds, watering the soil, and eventually, all his hard work pays off with the harvest. It's the same for the expert arrowhead hunter.

An expert artifact hunter spends years "preparing his soil". He travels many miles, kayaks many more, and keeps track of every campsite he locates. Eventually if weather cooperates and he gets his timing just right, all the hard work pays off and he harvests his arrowheads.

If you follow the techniques in this book, there really is no question that the artifacts will be there. Go get 'em.

"See your future. Be your future."--Ty Webb

Chapter 10: Archaeology & Ethics

The Politics of Arrowhead Hunting

When I first started hunting artifacts I joined my state archaeological society. I went into the office at my local university campus and signed up. At the time I was not aware of the politics of arrowhead hunting. I was not welcomed with open arms.

They looked at me with suspicious eyes when I asked if it was legal to hunt artifacts in public waterways. The girl in the office did her job by signing me up to the state archaeological society, taking my money, and explaining to me in no uncertain terms buying and selling of artifacts was wrong, digging was wrong, picking up artifacts from the river was legal but still wrong. Anyone who did any of those things was a pot hunter. I wasn't quite sure EXACTLY what a pot hunter was at that point, but based on their attitude I suspected it was something akin to a pedophile.

On a positive note, I would be receiving a quarterly publication in the mail whereby I could live vicariously through the articles of REAL ARCHAEOLOGISTS and might even be allowed to dig up artifacts with them once a year.

The bias against artifact collectors is systemic and has been institutionalized. Archaeology professors teach their students to paint all artifact collectors with a broad and negative brush from first year classes through graduate level. Students are taught that ANYONE buying and selling Indian artifacts is ignorant and malicious. The commercial market for arrowheads is the root cause of the entire problem according to professors.

Most archaeologists DO NOT LIKE (with extreme prejudice) arrowhead hunters and they use derogatory terms like "pot hunter" and "thieves of time" when referring to them. A pot hunter is someone who digs up archaeological sites in search of Indian artifacts without considering the permanent destruction of information contained within stratified deposits. While there are artifact collectors who deserve the title pot hunter and thief of time, these few bad apples do not represent the vast majority of ethical, honest artifact hunters and collectors who maintain a deep respect for ancient cultures.

Archaeology vs. Archaeologists
Archaeology is mostly one guy in a hole, digging out stuff and deciding what ways the stuff could have been used. Archaeology relies heavily on subjective speculation. This leads to phrases like "ceremonial object" which is archy code for "we have absolutely no idea." As a pure science,

archaeology and anthropology get little respect from academia. Consequently they get very little funding.

Despite their inherent flaws, anthropology and archaeology are the only means we have to study the origins and development of humanity. Personally, I love archaeology. Archaeologists………. maybe not so much. I used to think arrowhead hunters and archaeologists worked hand in hand, and helped each other figure out the mysteries of ancient man, but it turns out I was wrong.

Be careful when approaching archaeologists. They are not your friend. Archys are trained to put all arrowhead hunters in the same "thieves of time" category as the youtube cave diggers who actually deserve the title.

Most archaeologists are underpaid, underappreciated and very disgruntled. They are trapped between the ignorance the general public displays by digging up important sites, and the lack of available funds to pursue controlled digging of these same rare sites.

Any archaeologists who want their work taken seriously for peer review, or want to receive tenure in their field must CONFORM. If they don't agree with this negative stance toward arrowhead collectors, they will not be taken seriously by the rest of the herd, who will make them pay a great price. Taking a positive point of view on artifact collectors is career suicide for an archaeologist.

Clearly, archaeologists do not want anything to do with artifact hunters beyond using them to find significant sites.

The average archaeologist spends a couple weeks a year doing field work. This means they don't get out much. Most archys are not very skilled at surface hunting, or finding Indian campsites in the first place.

Archaeologists will badmouth arrowhead hunters, but do not hesitate to build their careers on the backs of these same amateurs. Archaeologists need to work with amateurs and the public. Arrowhead hunters get no credit for their contributions to the archaeological record today. If you read archaeological site reports from the 1950's, there was an obvious rapport between collectors and archys. That rapport has disappeared in modern times, and archaeology is suffering because of this adversarial relationship.

Typically, archaeologists don't discover Indian camps. They wait around their offices for some arrowhead hunter to bring them a couple of Daltons or Clovis points. Based on arrowhead hunters telling them where to go, they go out in the field and "discover" significant sites. Indiana Jones is a figment of our collective imagination. The current system has removed all adventure from archaeology, as well as most of the funding.

Most archaeologists are arrowhead collectors, and the vast majority of them have collections in their own homes--just for "research purposes," of course. Archaeologists will tell you people who buy and sell artifacts are the source of the problem, but that's not entirely accurate.

Archaeologists know the artifacts themselves have marginal value to science once their context has been studied. They know museums have all the arrowheads they will ever want. That leaves only artifact collectors as caretakers for these objects. Most artifacts eventually enter the commercial market. Museums often sell off artifacts to raise money, and museum donation is no guarantee of the fate of an artifact. Many long-time collectors donate their finds to museums only to have them sold off for cash by the museum. Reality is once artifacts are out of the ground, they are just a commodity from that point forward.

Caves and Rock Shelters are Special Places
The Real Science in Archaeology

While all archaeological digging is destructive, there is a difference in the goals of archaeologists and arrowhead hunters. Arrowhead hunters are only interested in finding arrowheads. For archaeologists the actual artifacts are secondary to what he can learn from context, comparison, stratified deposits, and carbon dating.

Carbon dating is a method used for determining the approximate age of an ancient object. The age is obtained by measuring the amount of carbon 14 contained within the sample. This process only works on samples that were once alive (charcoal, acorns, bones, leaves, etc.) and will not work on arrowheads. When intact layered deposits are present in archeological sites, biological samples found next to arrowheads are tested with the assumption both were deposited at the same time. In theory, the dates obtained from these biological samples will reflect the age of the stone artifact.

Unethical and Immoral Digging: Legitimate Beef with Arrowhead Hunters

Carbon dating is real science, as well as microscopic analysis of stone tool wear patterns, and the testing of blood residue found on projectile points, scrapers, and knives. This real science is most effectively performed on intact dry sites that contain biological samples and artifacts together. Dry caves and rock shelters are unique opportunities for studying ancient man. Uncontrolled digging of caves and shelters by amateurs results in permanent destruction of this truly irreplaceable information, and is unethical.

Even if you are unethical and don't care about destroying irreplaceable information, it is still immoral to dig caves and rock shelters. Caves and rock shelters contain human burials 90% of the time according to the archaeological record, and are considered graveyards. This means 9 out of 10 professionally excavated caves and shelters still contain human remains. This is not a guess. This is not speculation. Caves and shelters are graves.

Even the caves and rock shelters where no burials are found probably once contained them, but they have disintegrated over time. Uncontrolled digging in caves and rock shelters is unethical, immoral, and illegal in most cases.

Digging where graves are even LIKELY is illegal in most states. A 90% chance is definitely "likely." Many people don't like this, but there is no debate here. Caves and rock shelters are graves. You can have a different opinion, but your opinion doesn't change the facts.

However, not all sites are created equal. Rare Paleo-Indian sites, caves, and rock shelters should not be dug by amateurs. Other types of sites exist in such plentiful numbers that archaeologists choose not to dig them because they believe nothing new would be learned from the excavation.

Open sites dating from the archaic and woodland periods have been professionally excavated in great numbers. Digging more of these sites would probably not improve the body of knowledge in archaeology. In this grey area exists room for you to dig up the past without destroying information valuable to humanity.

If you are lucky enough to have an Indian camp on your private property, or permission from a landowner, digging is probably okay-if your state has no regulations against digging and does not require a permit. You can call your local archaeological society and ask about digging laws in your state. They might not be very cooperative, though!

Digging vs. Surface Hunting
To dig, or not to dig?

I have dug artifacts by hand and with heavy machinery in 5 different states. I could dig EVERY DAY if I wanted to, yet I find myself drawn to surface hunting over digging most of the time. For me, digging is a last resort. I usually don't consider digging until I have exhausted all other options. This is not because I am altruistic or any kind of hero. It's just that I find surface hunting a pure and rewarding experience. Surface hunting is spiritual, digging much more visceral. For me, a successful surface hunt is an accomplishment orders-of-magnitude beyond a successful dig, and I prefer hiking and kayaking to digging in a pit all day.

In the spirit of full disclosure, know that I have dug in all the wrong places before I knew better. Occasionally I still dig open sites and once a year I hit a Texas pay dig. Digging is the great equalizer. Experts and beginners have the same odds of finding something nice when digging artifacts in a known spot, but there are certain tools and techniques that will help you get more artifacts out of the ground. The real skill involved in digging is figuring out where to dig in the landscape. Beyond that it's mostly physical work and perseverance. There are a few arrowhead diggers in Texas who have made an ART of digging points, they seem to have a supernatural ability to move large volumes of dirt, and know exactly where to dig. But most people won't get the opportunity to dig enough to gain that level of skill.

This chapter on ethics purposely precedes the chapter on digging because digging is where ethics are relevant. There are legal considerations when surface hunting, but there are no moral or ethical considerations when surface hunting.

There is another difference between digging and surface hunting. When you find artifacts through surface hunting, you are RESCUING them from certain destruction. When you dig up artifacts, you are permanently destroying information inherent in their buried context. Therein lies the rub. Does this mean I won't dig anymore? No, I still go to Texas pay digs every year. I rationalize that these places are going to be dug anyway. Many landowners dig their own sites, and if they weren't digging them, these sites would probably never be discovered, and the artifacts never seen by humans at all, which mitigates the loss of context to a great degree.

Your safest bet for ethical digging is salvage digging on construction sites. If a site is in the process of being permanently destroyed through construction, there is no moral or ethical issue. If you can get in there and dig out some points, you are definitely rescuing them from certain destruction. Destruction of archaeological sites by construction is very common, and many times the presence of Indian artifacts is purposely overlooked by developers in favor of progress and profit.

Dig all you want, just remember to get landowner permission. There is no debate that 90 % of caves and rock shelters are graves, it's a fact. Open sites are your best bet to avoid grave digging. KNOW YOUR STATE LAWS FIRST. Other than that you are limited only by your conscience. If you want to dig caves and rock shelters with a clear conscience, don't read books. You can't unlearn what you don't like. OOPS, I guess it's too late for you!

Chapter 11: Digging the Past

Digging up the past can be rewarding but is a hell of a lot of work. If you want to dig up artifacts you need to have your own property or a landowner's permission. Never dig alone. Digging is inherently dangerous even without heavy machinery.

All digging is hazardous to your health, especially if the site is dry at the time you dig it. Collapsing pit walls and undercut tunnels suffocate many artifact diggers. Suffocation is a slow death that takes a good 5 minutes. However, there are worse things that can happen than a slow suffocation.

Ken and Hell's Fire
November 2009

About 10 years back a group of guys were digging a cave in Tennessee. They had been in the cave many times and recovered lots of nice artifacts. The four of them had become comfortable digging in there, probably a little too comfortable.

Ken was in his own pit 10' by 10' and about 8 feet deep. This pit had taken Ken several weekends to open up this large. He was using a Coleman kerosene lantern in the hole. Ken had been digging for hours and then "WHOOOOMP" a pit wall collapsed from one direction. He was only buried to his shoulders, so he wasn't going to suffocate. But he had fallen against his metal lantern hood when the pit collapsed, and began screaming immediately. You would think a buried Coleman lantern would go out from lack of oxygen. I suppose it was the loose dirt that allowed the lantern to remain lit.............

It took three of them over 10 minutes to dig him out. Ken's screams were described as tortured noises of the damned in hell. Ken was hospitalized with 3rd degree burns to his bone. This incident stayed with all of them for years, and they tell me it's just impossible to get it out of their head sometimes. Ken's lower leg was permanently disfigured.

Was this revenge of the Indian gods? I don't know. What I do know is that digging in caves is dangerous.

Willy B.

Fungus and mold spores in soil can infect you if breathed in while digging. Dried mouse urine becomes powdered and if you breathe it you will get Hanta virus, which can be fatal. If the site you are digging is dry at the time you dig, you should dig wearing a dust mask at a minimum. Charcoal filtered masks used in construction are preferred and much more comfortable. Western Safety makes a neoprene mask with charcoal filters and ear plugs built in, as well as a rubber exhaust valve. These Western Safety masks are washable and even come with replacement filters.

You are probably OK without a mask if you are digging open field sites and the ground is wet. Digging dry ground means breathing in the dust, and there will always be a risk breathing in dirt and organic material.

Caves and Rock Shelters

DO NOT DIG CAVES AND ROCK SHELTERS. Caves and shelters are graveyards. If you have no problem digging up dead Indians that's your business, but it's BAD JUJU. Lots of caves and rock shelters get dug, but the funny thing is, in many cases artifacts inside a cave or shelter will not be as plentiful as those buried right in front of it.

I have spent the night in caves and rock shelters, and it's not a pleasant experience. Only bad weather or safety concerns forced Indians into caves voluntarily. It's much more pleasant outside, right in front of a rock shelter or cave, and this is where the bulk of daytime activities occurred in warm weather. My own experience is you will find a LOT more stuff over a much wider area by digging in front of cave entrances and rock shelters.

In this way you can still recover artifacts from cave or rock shelter sites, hopefully without disturbing graves or digging dry deposits.

People have been digging caves and shelters for a long time, and you will hear people say "that shelter is all dug out." For the most part this is just not true. Amateurs will dig a shelter and pile the sift dirt outside, right in front of the drip line. Many times underneath this pile of sift dirt is a treasure trove of artifacts.

Ollie's Treasure Pit--October 2010

My buddy Ollie dug a field in front of a rock shelter in Kentucky most weekends for several years. The landowner had dug out the rock shelter to bedrock many years earlier and recovered about one hundred nice points. Ollie and the landowner were digging in the field in front of the shelter. They were digging by hand and finding several artifacts each time they dug for a few hours. Some days they would come up empty handed, but they were finding enough stuff to make it interesting.

They were a good 100 feet out into the field in front of the shelter, and came across an interesting feature while digging. A layer of clay soil about 3 feet under the grass-line had been compacted really well. It was the kind of thing that would happen if you were camping on the open ground every day and using the same small spot over and over. This compacted clay soil encompassed an area about 15 feet square.

Ollie soon discovered a small grass-lined pit within this larger feature. The clay pit was about 18 inches in diameter. They saw points sticking out of the top of the pit and were very excited. This entire grass lined pit was full of artifacts. It contained 237 medium and large turkey-tail points made from blue/grey hornstone! There were more artifacts in that one small feature than in the entire rock shelter itself.

Willy B.

Not all caves and rock shelters contain artifacts. Caves and shelters that face south are the best bets for having artifacts buried inside them (and thereby in front of them for our purposes). Camping inside rock shelters and caves is truly miserable. It's kind of like camping on the beach. You get sand in every crevice. Unless it's cold or you are being physically threatened by humans or animals, you don't want to be inside a cave. It's dark in there. You can't do much effectively by firelight. Even knapping arrowheads is difficult by firelight (I tried it!). Consequently you need sunlight. In North America this means your cave or shelter entrance needs to face SOUTH. South facing entrances allow the sun to light-up and warm-up your space.

Digging a Spring

If you have a spring on your land you can try digging IN the spring itself. This technique only works if you have a good sized rocky pool right where the water comes out of the ground. I have recovered very nice artifacts using this method. You have to dig with a shovel. Get down into the spring source pool and shovel the rocks into a floating sifter, then search them for arrowheads. Even in summer this will be a COLD EXPERIENCE! My spring is 58 degrees year round. Wear neoprene chest waders or a wetsuit. In my particular spring artifacts started showing up two feet below the top of the gravel. Once you go through the rocks in the sifter, dump them outside the pool. I don't know why the artifacts are here, but most of them I find in springs are whole, like they were stashed here purposely.

It is also possible to dig right next to a spring pool and come up with some nice artifacts. I can picture Indians sitting on the edge of the spring pool on hot summer days, feet in the water, making arrowheads. Any high spots near a spring should be investigated for flint flakes and camp rocks. Dig some test holes 2 feet square on these high spots. If you come up with camp sign (flint flakes and camp rocks), KEEP DIGGING!

Digging Field Sites
A plowed field that produces arrowheads should be dug with a plan. Random digging of a large acreage is pretty much pointless (no pun intended). Every plowed field will have areas of concentrated habitation. We want to locate these areas and dig there, hopefully uncovering deposits that exist below the plow zone. Areas that show a higher concentration of flint flakes and artifacts are what field hunters refer to as "hot spots." If you are not already familiar with these areas of occupation in your field; plow it, wait for rain, and hot spots will make themselves obvious.

These hot spots are where you will dig your test trenches. Many fields have been plowed for 100 years and the plow zone is full of mostly damaged artifacts. You must dig below this 18 inch plow zone to check your field for intact artifact deposits.

You could do this with a shovel, but it will take you days to dig a hole the size you need to see what is down there. You need a backhoe to do it right. A trench one bucket wide, 20 feet long, and six feet deep, right through the heart of your best hotspot is a great place to start. Check the dirt piles first for flint flakes and artifacts. Then jump down in the trench and look at the walls. Camp deposits are darker areas that contain charcoal, ash, fire rocks, flint flakes, and artifacts. These deposits are in layers with the oldest deposits below newer ones, and all deposits exhibit themselves as dark brown or black lines of varying thicknesses. These ash and rock deposits are referred to as "fire pits" and archys call them "lenses" because they tend to be thicker in the center and taper thin toward the edges.

Dig into these discolored areas with your wiggle pick (see tools section). If you start finding flint flakes you are onto something! If there are no discolorations you should dig a little anyway just to be sure, at least a couple of feet into the wall at a position below the plow zone. If you find nothing, fill the hole in, and check your next hot spot. You should check all your hot spots before eliminating the field.

Once you find flint flakes you can dig by hand in your pit walls. Personally I prefer hand digging over machine digging and find it much more rewarding. Dig the dark areas first as these are generally more lucrative. However, it's a lot quicker to use the backhoe, which requires a large table sifter (see tools section below).

Be careful when checking trench walls, they could collapse and trap you. It's best to have another person there in case something goes wrong. Bystanders need to keep clear of heavy machinery and be far enough back to avoid the arc of a swinging bucket arm. Enlarge your trench to at least a couple bucket widths if you intend to hand dig pit walls for an extended time. This allows a margin of safety against pit wall collapse.

Sometimes hand digging test holes is your only option. If you are hand digging test holes, knowing where to dig is not the only consideration. When it's hot and dry using a shovel is nearly impossible in most places. The ground is just too hard, and requires a pick axe just to start your hole. You will have to wait until a good rain soaks the ground to make digging with hand tools possible.

You can overcome rock hard soil conditions by watering the area you intend to dig with a thorough soaking before attempting to hand dig. Most Indian camps have a water source nearby. A five gallon bucket will serve you well as a field expedient method of wetting hard ground. Once you get a foot or two deep you will find digging much easier.

Tools for Hand Digging
There is no better tool for just moving dirt by hand than a good old number 2 shovel. I have recovered nice artifacts digging with a shovel, but it's easy to damage them. There is no worse sound than the edge of a flint artifact being crushed by steel.

There are as many types of digging tools as there are people who dig, but one stands out above all others: the Texas wiggle pick. I first saw one of these amazing tools on a pay dig site in Texas. This tool looks like a pick axe with a pick blade on one side only, and a 20 inch handle. The blade has proportions like a 10 inch double-edged dagger. If used properly a wiggle pick will allow you to move large amounts of dirt in an Indian camp without damaging artifacts. Shovels are best relegated to removing overburden and opening test pits. Once you get your pit opened, time to pull out the wiggle pick.

First you insert the tip of your wiggle pick blade into the wall of an already open trench. You should choose areas that are darker brown or black, indicating presence of decayed organic matter from Indian occupation. You push the sharp tip into the wall using your body weight. By wiggling the handle as you push, the soil is compressed, which makes room for the blade to slip into the dirt. As you push SLOWLY into the wall, listen for contact with flint rock. You will hear and FEEL any contact with stone. If you hit stone, pull out the pick and reposition it few inches away, starting over again until you can insert the full length of the blade without contacting stone. This allows you to AVOID breaking nice artifacts that may be present.

Once you have the blade fully inserted into the wall, you use the handle to lever large chunks of soil out of the wall. Allow these chunks of soil to fall onto the floor of your trench. You will then use your hands to push apart these chunks, revealing any flint chips, camp rocks, or artifacts. Wiggle picks are truly amazing pieces of equipment and can be obtained from online sources. Mountain climbers use a tool called an ICE AXE or and ICE ADZE that is nearly identical to a wiggle pick.

Texas Pay Digs

Some Texas ranches have been in operation for 40 years as pay dig arrowhead camps. These old time camps are cratered like the moon over large acreages. Generally you pay between $40 and $125 per day for 8 hours of hand digging. Price depends on how lucrative the camp is. If you are incapable of digging or just don't want to dig, backhoe digs are $200 for an eight hour day. You will get all the camp dirt you can push through a sifter table brought right to you for $200 a day.

When I talk about Texas pay digs, it never fails that somebody will suggest these digs are fraudulent and the points are planted. That is just complete nonsense spewed out by people with no first first-hand experience. I assure you pay digs in Texas are real, and artifacts are not salted or fake. These digs are full of fire cracked limestone rocks that fall apart as they are being removed. It would not be possible to set that up. Also, I find too much stuff for it to be economical to have fakes made at the prices they charge.

On hand dig camps, they open a trench usually 6 feet deep. Paying customers are allowed to dig in these walls (or anywhere else for that matter) and keep anything they find. Yes, it's all real, and yes, it is possible to find some really nice artifacts. It's also possible to end up with nothing (mostly from not trying very hard). You pay your money either way.

These pay digs advertise and most allow camping for a fee. Some are on ranches that have cabins for rent. Search the internet for Texas arrowhead pay digs. I have been to 7 different pay digs in Texas over the last 7 years. Every single one was a fantastic experience well worth the price. Be prepared to work hard if you want good results, even when backhoe digging. Pushing dirt through a sifter screen all day will wear you out, too. Bring your own tools and come with a strategy. I have dug up some WORLD CLASS artifacts at these places.

Pay Dig Strategy: Quick and Dirty

You want to move the most dirt in the least amount of time from locations that give you the best chance of producing arrowheads. Using this technique means the difference between finding something good and going home empty handed. You only have 8 hours to dig and this may be your only opportunity if you drive from out of state. Do what needs to be done to produce some good artifacts and don't worry about being thorough.

G10 Texas Pay Dig Points dug by the author. Left to Right: A root beer flint Perd, a super thin 4 5/8" Friday knife, and a 4" Nolan.

On many sites there is a layer of overburden that contains no artifacts. Removing overburden is a waste of your limited time. In pay dig sites you "high grade" the pit wall with your pick, choosing darker stained areas that indicate artifact deposits. Dig in these "pay layers" creating an undercut. Be careful not to dig too deep into the wall, any farther than 3 feet is very dangerous. If you undercut too deep, the overburden will collapse on your head. Dig into a pit wall 3 feet, then move to a new spot and start again.

It takes too much time to sift your dirt when hand-digging at pay dig sites. Any small artifacts missed will not be worth the time it takes to bring the dirt over to a sifter table. Remove large chunks of soil from the pit wall and let them drop to the floor of the pit. Sometimes the soil is really hard and you will have difficulty breaking the chunks apart. Place one gloved hand on the soil chunk and use your body weight to push it apart. Expect to do a lot of work if you want good results.

This method of pushing apart chunks of soil with your hands, checking the dirt visually, and then repeating the process leaves a big mess. You will miss some artifacts occasionally. The mess you leave behind is not your concern at a pay dig. Just keep digging, dropping chunks, and looking through them, hell bent for leather.

I can last as long as my gloved hands will allow. Usually this is a two day limit, which works out well as I rarely get more than two days on any given pay dig travelling from out of state. Many times I have left pay digs with swollen hands and fingers that no longer work. I am then forced to drive home using only my thumbs and 4 non-operational fingers. We call this "driving home with the claw" and wear this condition proudly as if it were a war wound.

If you are expecting an easy day digging, think again. Be prepared to WORK HARD if you want to find something nice. I have dug at places with 10 other diggers, and 6 of them will go home with nothing, because they give up and don't want to do any real work. If you want arrowheads the easy way, go to an artifact show and buy some. There is no easy way to find arrowheads.

Digging Your Own Land
Slow and Thorough

When digging your own site you have all the time you want and you should do a MUCH more thorough job. This requires sifting all campsite dirt to recover small projectiles, and other artifacts. You will find artifacts outside of the lens shaped, dark colored deposits. SIFT ALL DIRT. Through trial and error you will find the depth limits of the deposits in your field. Basically you dig until you stop finding flint flakes and artifacts. Then you know how deep to dig the other holes. This can be tricky though.

Many sites were not continuous occupations. Sometimes there will be a sterile layer of soil between deposits of artifacts. This layer can be 1 to 8 feet thick in my experience. A sterile layer indicates a length of time when the site went unoccupied. You might have a deposit 3 feet down that produces artifacts from the woodland period (maybe 2000 years old). Then you could have a sterile layer 5 feet thick that won't even have a single flint flake in it, indicating no Indians were present for many thousands of years. Under that sterile layer there could be an early archaic deposit producing artifacts 7,000 years old.   Not all sites were occupied at all times. Sites with deposits from different time periods are called multi-component sites.

Digging below archaic deposits can produce even older paleo-Indian deposits. These oldest deposits can be 10,000 years old but are very rare. It's usually not worth digging deeper than archaic levels, because you will see very spotty results for the amount of dirt you have to search. There just weren't as many Indians around in the paleo times, and they moved around a lot following game herds (their main food source). During middle and late archaic times the development of agriculture allowed Indians to have more sedentary lifestyles. Because archaic and woodland Indians had more food, there were greater populations; which translates to larger deposits containing more artifacts.

Sifter Screens
Sifters come in all shapes and sizes depending on your needs. There are small portable sifters built on wooden frames with backpack straps for hiking into difficult areas. Some sifters are made to float for use in a spring or lake.   At a pay dig or private dig site there are often steel or wooden framed sifter tables measuring 4 by 8 feet. These sifter tables usually have expanded steel or square wire mesh.

For smaller portable screens a minimum effective size is 18 inches square with 3 or 4 inch high sides to keep the dirt in while you shake the sifter and push dirt through. Building your own sifters is fun and you will improve your designs over time. Mesh size should be 3/8 of an inch unless you are in a woodland age camp that produces lots of small arrow points. In a woodland period camp a 1/4 inch mesh is more appropriate.

You want a floating sifter for digging springs and sifting creek gravel. Build your sifter frame, add your mesh, and then attach sections of foam water noodles to the sides for flotation. You can use zip ties to attach the water noodles. If you are shoveling into your floating sifter while standing in moving water, you need a rope tied around your waist attached to your sifter. This will keep your sifter from floating away with water currents.

Small portable sifters can be hung by ropes from tree branches allowing them to be swung back and forth greatly reducing effort required to get the dirt through them. If there are no trees you can build a large tripod using wooden poles 10 or 12 feet long.

On large sifter tables it is helpful to use small plastic garden shovels about a foot long to help you push dirt through the screen without damaging artifacts. Gloves are mandatory for pushing dirt through a sifter. Without gloves you will get cut. Your hands become tender after a full day of doing this, even if you wear the gloves and use a small plastic shovel.

A friend of mine digs artifacts for a living and has his own 4 by 8 foot steel framed sifter tables. The tables are covered with expanded steel mesh, and have electric vibration units attached underneath them. These vibration units are run by gas powered generators right in the field. This is the ultimate setup, the dirt falls through the screen on its own and you don't even need to do much pushing. These "ultimate sifter tables" even have sled runners built under them so they can be easily repositioned.

Artifact Mining
Efficient Use of Heavy Machinery

You can mine artifacts by yourself but it will be excruciatingly slow. Ideally artifact mining with heavy machinery is done on your own private property, with family members and friends. It can however, be done as a business proposition. Either way you will need a crew to do it right. You need to be able to trust each crew member. It would be easy for any crew member to pocket artifacts without others knowing, and some small artifacts can be VERY VALUABLE.

Commercial artifact mining has been successfully accomplished in Tennessee, Texas, Kentucky, and Missouri by myself and a few others. I am sure it could be done in other states. The limiting factor is state law. Many states do not allow digging on ANY archaeological sites, even ones on YOUR OWN PRIVATE PROPERTY! Be sure you know what you are doing and fully understand local laws if you want to do this.

Getting ready to open a hole in Tennessee.

Most times we do these digs by leasing land under written contract with a local farmer. We have paid up to $15,000 for a 12 month lease on a particularly lucrative camp. Lease costs are split by the crew, who are equal partners. All artifacts are considered community property. Artifacts are collected and sent to high end auctions. Proceeds from the auctions are used to pay off the lease and equipment costs, including backhoe rental and even gas. All artifacts are collected and sold until the break-even point is hit. After the break even point, artifacts are split at the end of each day on a rotating basis and each person does what he wants with his share of the points. Some keep them all, and some people sell them to pay their bills. Yes, it is possible to dig artifacts on a professional basis, although I am aware of only 2 people in all of North America who do this successfully full time. One thing that's guaranteed about making a living, it's a LOT of work, no matter how you do it.

If a single artifact is particularly valuable, it is usually sold for money and split between partners, even after the break-even point is reached. If one partner wants to keep a high end piece, a value is estimated and that person must relinquish as many of his own artifacts as it takes to equal the value of a really high end piece. For example, a slate winged bannerstone recovered at a site in Kentucky sold for $8,000.

It is unusual to recover such valuable pieces, but if one of us had wanted to keep it, he would have to relinquish artifacts of equal value from arrowheads in his possession.

Mechanics of Mining

You can go bobcat style or backhoe style. The advantage lies with backhoes, unless one of your partners already owns a bobcat. Renting heavy equipment is generally too expensive, although we have leased old backhoes from farmers for as little as $500 per month! If you lease an old backhoe be prepared to deal with hydraulic leaks, and have extra hydraulic fluid on hand. We have been able to keep old diggers running with gorilla tape and hillbilly ingenuity, but this isn't for everyone. You are best served buying a good used small to medium backhoe and then selling it when you are done. Typically you can buy a small one for 8 or 10 thousand dollars.

Bobcat Style Digs

Small to medium backhoes are the preferred equipment, although a bobcat will do if you are skilled. The main limitation with a bobcat is opening the pit in the first place. With a bobcat style dig you will have to open up a HUGE pit at least 8 feet deep. Use the front end loader to remove a bucket load at a time, which is then delivered to multiple sifter tables in an ongoing basis. This means you will have a GIANT pit open for the duration of the dig, and it will expand every day. Sift dirt will be collected from screen piles at the end of each day and piled up next to your pit. When you reach the limits of a given occupation, then the dirt is pushed back in and the pit is filled.

Backhoe Style Digs

Most landowners are much more comfortable with backhoe style digs, as you generally start a new pit each day and fill it in at the end of the day. This style of dig does not require huge pits and is cleaner looking for landowners, as well as being safer. Your backhoe will remain at ground level, and you won't have to travel up and down dirt ramps, which can be very dangerous.

While it is possible to dig camp dirt with an articulated backhoe arm and drop each bucket on the sifter table individually, this is not an efficient method. Sifter tables positioned right next to the pit create danger for the sifting crew.

Ideally the front end loader on the backhoe drops a cubic yard at a time on sifter tables. Then the backhoe goes back to the pit and continues digging with its arm. The backhoe operator uses the digging arm to pile dirt next to his open pit, and keeps on digging until he notices the sifter table is empty or is signaled by the sifting crew. When the table is empty the backhoe operator stops digging, locks down the digging arm and spins around in his seat. Then he uses the front end loader to pick up a cubic yard of dirt from his pile which he delivers to the nearby sifter table. DO NOT drop an entire bucket of dirt onto a sifter table all at once. A cubic yard of dirt weighs 2,000 pounds or more! Drop the dirt SLOWLY. The sifter tables should be positioned close enough for the backhoe driver to have a visual, but far enough away that no safety issue is created for the sifting crew.

Commercial lease operations are time sensitive. You need to get as many artifacts out of the ground as quickly as you can to keep the whole thing going. It's really, really amazing when you get this all worked out correctly.

Sifting crews work in pairs, two men to each table. Using two tables is the most efficient set up. The cycle is dig the hole, fill the table, sift the dirt. Then repeat until the dirt under the sifting table touches the underside of the sifting screens. The sifter tables are pushed away from the dirt piles by the sifting crews. This opens up new space under the tables. The backhoe just continues until everyone needs a break, usually 2 or 3 hours. This has the effect of leaving piles of sifted dirt right next to each other spaced equally in the field. At the end of the day the backhoe pushes the sift dirt back into the pit and fills it up.

Sometimes we are forced to dig at night because of 100 degree daytime temperatures. We use generators to power large construction lights. It's quite a sight to see all this lit up at night, with a crew of people working in teams over multiple sifter tables while a backhoe digs furiously to keep the tables full of dirt. A good crew quickly becomes a well-oiled machine.

I have been on many different types of job sites in my life, and arrowhead mines are unlike any of them. Only on artifact mining sites is EVERY MAN SMILING ALL DAY AND NIGHT. You will literally dig until your body quits and you are forced to go home. Anyone who is forced to leave and take care of other responsibilities is not happy. It's kind of crazy, really. But you want to try it, don't you?

Limiting Breakage

It is AMAZING how small the amount of breakage is when digging artifacts with heavy machinery. During one 6 month lease only 8 artifacts were destroyed by heavy machinery, and hundreds of arrowheads were recovered.

Mostly the backhoe operator will not see any artifacts. However, occasionally something large pokes out or caches of stacked artifacts are revealed. In these instances the backhoe driver stops his backhoe, and recovers these finds safely. On particularly lucrative camps, it pays to have an extra guy just watching for points while the backhoe digs.

Chapter 12: Documenting Your Finds
In-Situ Photographs

IN-SITU: Being in the original position. Not having been moved or transferred to another location. Taking a picture of an artifact BEFORE you move it is an in-situ photograph.

Overall in-situ photo, point is bottom center. You want to show context, but be careful not to show any landmarks that give away your location.

Close up in-situ photo. It's unusual for artifacts to be "tombstoned" like this. This campsite is under 9 feet of water in normal conditions.

In hand photo. WOW. G10 chisel tipped Dickson with orange lake stain.

I enjoy these pictures almost as much as the artifacts themselves. Sometimes it's difficult to remember to stop and take a picture, but it's very rewarding. This is another hobby within the hobby for me, and I take lots of pictures on all my hunts.

Proper documentation is a three-step process. You want to take an overall shot showing the context of the find, a close-up in-situ shot, and an in-hand shot to show size of the artifact. When you take a photo with an artifact in your hand, steady your hand against something solid. Steadying your hand will allow the camera to maintain focus and your pictures will turn out better.

In-situ series photos REALLY capture the moment. When I look at these pictures it's like re-living the experience all over again!

You will need an outdoor camera or cellphone/camera that is waterproof and shockproof. If you take your regular camera you are just asking for trouble. I have lost 2 camera's from dropping them in water (2 phones as well). I finally broke down and bought a waterproof shockproof cell phone with a built in high quality camera. Anything 5 mega pixel or better will take great photos outdoors in sunlight.

Casio makes a line of cell phones built to military specifications and they are pretty much indestructible. Casio phones will take pictures under water. They have a removable micro-sd card that allows me to easily upload these photos to my computer. I can also print pictures out at any photo kiosk using the micro-sd card.

You won't have a problem getting good pictures outdoors in full sunlight with a cell phone camera. I took all of the outdoor pictures in this book with a Casio cell phone camera!

Overall photo. Notice the snow on the bank. I am wearing my lucky winter hat, and a smile money can't buy!

Close up in-situ above, and an in-hand shot right.

Good sized point with a neat brown inclusion at its center. Photographing your finds at home is best accomplished with the use of a tripod to steady the camera. Most cameras have a macro setting. Macro setting is used to take close up pictures. Macro setting works well, but requires you to move the lens within inches of the object to get a

REALLY close shot of tiny bird points. Cameras cannot focus when you get too close.

Macro zoom and indirect light used to take a photo of an arrowhead 3/8 of an inch long!

I used the grass to steady my hand for this photo of a large Sedalia point with a hole through it.

G9 Williams drill found in a plowed field in 2010.

Really good cameras have a macro zoom. This allows you to stay back a foot or so away from the object being photographed, and zoom in to fill the entire frame. You can use indirect light to accentuate the flaking patterns on an artifact.

Digital pictures taken with a smart phone are a great way to document your hunt. But some smart phones are a little too smart. The date and location of photos are automatically recorded by internal GPS on many models of smart phones, and they will send coordinates along with picture text messages. You need to disable this function or you will be giving away your best spots if you send a picture text of your in-situ.

The Apple i-phone will automatically populate google maps with your photos using GPS coordinates, showing the entire world what you found on a full color map available to the general public. You must turn this feature off or it can happen automatically. You could use this feature from the other direction. Go search google maps and look for in-situ pictures of artifacts along creeks and rivers!

Artifact Hunting Videos

It's a lot of fun to make your own video. Some people even post these videos on youtube. It's perfectly acceptable to make your own videos. BUT, I do not recommend posting artifact videos on the internet. It's too easy to give away your hunting spots. They say a picture is worth a thousand words, and that's a lot of information. A video has 30 still pictures in each SECOND. Be careful posting videos on the internet, or even posting still pictures. Do not post overall shots that have landmarks in the background. Many people have lost hunting spots because they posted photos and videos online. In takes YEARS to find out which creeks and riverbanks have artifacts in them. When you post a video or photo on the internet you are placing an advertisement giving the exact location of your Indian campsite. If you INSIST on posting photos or videos, keep the shot tight on the artifact. Do not even show a tree if it has identifiable characteristics. If you show any landmarks, someone will find your site, and you will be VERY UNHAPPY.

Some people dig caves and rock shelters, video the dig, and post it on youtube. Some youtube cave diggers claim they just want to "share the experience" with others, some are in it for the money, and they sell their finds on personal websites, using the videos to advertise to buyers. Some are obviously filming cave digging for the cheap thrill of getting youtube hits. No matter which of these three reasons a youtube cave digger posts cave or rock shelter digging videos, they are publicly damaging the reputation of ALL arrowhead hunters, and encouraging new anti-collector regulations and laws. Digging caves and shelters is unethical, and can be illegal, and a video of you doing this may not be in your best interest.

Cave and rock shelter digging videos have the effect of encouraging the general public to dig up rare archaeological sites for fun and profit. These videos give ammunition to archaeologists in their fight to pass laws making arrowhead hunting illegal, even surface hunting. Those who post cave or rock shelter digging on youtube are providing evidence and credence for use of the derogatory terms "thief of time" and "pot hunter".

Chapter 13: Artifact Hunting Safety

Personal safety is my NUMBER ONE concern every time I leave the house to go arrowhead hunting. Artifact hunters of every age and experience level die each year while out trying to find arrowheads. Many drown, some fall off bluffs, and some get lost and die from exposure to heat or cold. The first time you don't take safety seriously could be your last.

In January of 2013 a 35 year old father and his two sons aged 8 and 10 died after getting lost hiking in the woods in Missouri. It was 60 degrees when they left and they were wearing light clothing. They were on a marked trail, but lost their bearings and ended up spending the night outside, which they were not prepared for. The dad was an Air Force veteran and an experienced hiker, but he was not prepared for the 2 inch rainstorm and 35 degree temperatures. It doesn't matter if you have been doing something for years, if you aren't prepared for the worst, you will die when the worst happens.

Before You Leave the House
You should hunt with a partner when possible. It can mean the difference between life and death. A hunting partner can get help to you if you tumble down a mountain or pull you out of the water if you fall off a cut-bank and knock yourself out. Unfortunately it's not always possible to get someone to go along. Hunting by yourself can be accomplished safely if you follow some simple rules.

When you hunt alone it is important to leave detailed information with someone you trust. Include enough information to allow a search party to find you. Write down where you park your vehicle, plus your general plan, and when you will be back. Leave this information with a family member. This is the only way searchers will know where to go look for you if you don't return home. If you think this is not necessary, think again. NEVER go hunting alone without leaving DETAILED information where you are going and when you will be back.

Your next consideration is safety equipment. Rivers and lakes are EXTREMELY DANGEROUS and should not be taken lightly. As soon as you get too comfortable, you will die. There are a hundred ways to die hunting arrowheads.

You can fall on the slippery river rocks, hit your head and drown in 12 inches of water. You could cut yourself on broken glass and bleed to death right there. Do you have the means to survive even one cold rainy night if you break your leg and can't hike out of the forest? What happens if you get lost? If a pack of wild dogs surrounds you, what would you do? Cell phones are great, but ultimately not reliable. Cell phones can be broken, lost, or run out of batteries. In remote areas you might not even get a signal.

You need to carry a survival kit even when going on short hikes, and even more extensive equipment when boating. Should you become incapacitated, you need to have enough survival gear to stay alive until help comes.

Minimum Safety Equipment

I never leave home without everything on this list; NEVER. The life you save may be your own. I use a small backpack for my survival supplies, water, and lunch.

WATER- Enough water for 24 hours. I use an insulated stainless steel quart bottle. More if it's hot outside.

FOOD- I pack a lunch for day hikes, but carry limited emergency supplies like shelled pistachios and dried cherries. Trail mix or beef jerky make excellent backup foods. I eat DEER JERKY after hunting season. Deer jerky is REAL Indian food. The secret to good deer jerky is to wash out the thin-cut strips of venison with a water hose about 6 times before drying it, this gets the blood out. Then apply a nice spicy dry rub and dry it in a food dehydrator.

CELL PHONE- Fully charged with an extra fully charged battery. Extra batteries are cheap and lightweight. I prefer waterproof shock resistant cell phone models by Casio. An Apple i-phone in an otter box will NOT cut the mustard. If you have to carry a conventional cell phone get a waterproof Pelican box, the type with a rubber gasket that latches closed, and keep your phone and extra battery inside.

Be aware that in remote areas you will not always get a consistent signal. When you lose your cell phone signal, your phone will automatically and continuously seek a signal. This uses the same amount of battery juice as making a phone call. You can rapidly deplete your phone's battery in only a couple of hours when this happens. It's best to turn your cell phone off while hiking, in order to preserve your battery for emergency use.

EMERGENCY WHISTLE- This helps you attract the attention of search parties. I have a light weight red plastic tube with a BB in it. This little red tube sounds like a SIREN when you blow in it.

SPACE BLANKET- If you get caught outdoors overnight this can save your life. The BAG type space blankets are even better because you can get inside them. A space blanket would have saved the lives of the lost hiker and his two sons.

MAGNESIUM FIRE STARTER KIT- One of these can start a fire even in the rain with wet wood. The kit consists of a magnesium block and a striker bar. You shave small pieces off the block with the back of your knife in a pile about the size of a quarter. Then use the back of your knife on the striker bar to make sparks directly on your pile of magnesium shavings. These shavings burn at 4000 degrees and will even start wet wood. DO NOT BUY CHEAP CHINESE MADE MAGNESIUM KITS. These Chinese knock-offs DO NOT WORK and are completely WORTHLESS. Buy military issue DOANS MANUFACTURING magnesium fire starters. You should pay about $10 for a good DOANS magnesium fire starter. TEST YOUR GEAR. Start a fire with one of these AHEAD OF TIME. If you don't know how to use it, it's no good to you. A good military issue DOANS magnesium bar would have saved the lives of the Air Force hiker and his two sons.

BANDAIDS and POLYSPORIN- Used for small cuts and abrasions. River water contains bacteria and parasitic organisms. Treat any cuts IMMEDIATELY.

IBUPROFEN and TYLENOL- I like to carry 2 ibuprofen and 2 Tylenol.

TOILET PAPER- I keep this in a small waterproof bag. TP is definitely survival gear!

BEAR MACE- My personal choice for warding off predators. It has a 20 foot range and is lighter than carrying a handgun.

LIGHTWEIGHT HANDGUN- Optional, but almost every hunter I know carries one. Have you ever seen the movie DELIVERANCE?

STAINLESS STEEL KNIFE- I carry a fixed blade Buck knife on my hip.

SNAKE BITE KIT- If you have venomous snakes in your area you need one of these. If you get bitten, REMAIN CALM. Panic will only spread the venom more quickly. Read and understand the instructions in your snake bite kit BEFORE you need to use it. TEST YOUR GEAR.

PATROL MAP and COMPASS- A hand drawn map of the area. Even experienced people get lost sometimes. It pays to carry a lightweight compass when hiking. They don't need batteries like your GPS and cell phone.

BINOCULARS- Good for spotting landmarks. Small lightweight nitrogen filled model. These aren't NECESSARY, but I always carry them and often use them. It's good to be able to SEE who might be heading in your direction, and if they are armed. In deep woods I avoid other people as a general rule.

LIGHTER- For quickly starting fires under dry conditions. You can use a lighter to start your magnesium shavings quickly. When it's dry, I use leaves and twigs as kindling.

PORTABLE ARROWHEAD FRAME- This is a small Pelican waterproof box with a foam insert. This will keep you from losing or damaging any arrowheads you find. Definitely survival gear-arrowhead survival, anyway! Once you lose or break a nice arrowhead in the field, you will never leave home without a portable arrowhead frame.

GORILLA TAPE- Ten feet rolled up on itself. This stuff can do anything, it's the ultimate duct tape. If you get a hole in your kayak this tape is the best temporary fix. Gorilla tape will stay on your hull underwater for miles. You can use it to build a shelter if you get lost and have to stay in the woods overnight. You can use it to make field dressings and apply direct pressure if you cut yourself seriously. This stuff is LEGENDARY. Don't leave home without it.

Hunt Report
That Sinking Feeling....
June 2011

I took a buddy of mine kayaking for the first time today. He is an experienced field and creek hunter, but has never kayaked before today. We drove 15 miles away to the nearest federally navigable river. This is my home river and I know it real well. There are 5 sites in the 3.5 mile stretch, but we only managed to hunt 3 of them (we ran out of time).

We bypassed most gravel bars and cut-banks, going straight for the meat of known sites. The river was low and my plan was to hunt the middle of the main channel where it's only 2 feet deep, below cut-banks that produce arrowheads.

The problem was, a mile downstream I cracked my old sun-hardened kayak on a big rock. I was taking on water quickly. We pulled to the side on a gravel bar. There was a three inch crack directly under the seat. This meant I could not tape it inside and out like I normally would for a hull puncture. I have to dry the boat thoroughly before applying the Gorilla Tape. After emptying the water, and waiting a few minutes for the crack to dry thoroughly, I put GORILLA TAPE on the now dry bottom of the kayak. Gorilla tape is magic. It stayed on underwater for 2.5 miles. No leaks for the rest of the trip.

We continued with the hunt, and my buddy found a broken drill on the next gravel bar. I was hunting the main channel as I had planned. Then in the water, in the middle of the main channel, where it's only knee deep, I saw a base sticking out from the gravel.

If it was a point, I figured it was probably broke. I called my buddy over to check it out. I took a couple of in-situ shots, but the current was moving and I couldn't get the camera to focus. I dug the rocks from below the base while my buddy watched. It kept getting longer. There couldn't be a tip on it......

My first whole Dalton!

I was so happy I couldn't concentrate on finding points the rest of the day. I

checked my portable frame twice to make sure it was real and really in there.

My friend found the next two and learned how to kayak while I paddled around in a daze—awesome day on the river.

Happy Hunting
Willy B.

My basic survival kit.

Special Warnings and Gear

The river is a very dangerous environment. Be deliberate in your movements and be careful where you step, especially in slippery river rocks and on river banks. Walking in the river bottom is an accident waiting to happen. Falling down in the river is inevitable-plan for it. A walking stick is very helpful when negotiating slippery river bottoms. A walking stick gives you a third point of contact to steady yourself.

Be sure to tie your boat up or pull small boats completely out of the water. Boats can blow away from the shoreline or riverbank on windy days, setting them adrift and leaving you stranded.

SUMMER CONSIDERATIONS

Heat stress can kill you. If it's over 90 degrees plan to hunt IN THE WATER. Get in the water and stay there most of the day. Take double your normal amount of drinking water. I use stainless steel water bottles with an insulated neoprene cover. Fill your water bottles with ice cubes at home before filling them up with water.

I don't like sunscreen all over me, so I wear long sleeve vented fishing shirts and a fishing hat that shades my ears and neck. In a kayak, sun will reflect off the water and burn you, even if you are wearing a large brim fishing hat. You will need sunscreen on your face and neck even if you are wearing a long sleeve fishing shirt. Buy fishing shirts rated with a sun protection factor, an ordinary t-shirt offers little protection from UV rays and you will get burned right through it. All my fishing shirts have an SPF 30 rating right on the tag when I buy them. Your shirt and hat should be white, or at least light colored. It makes a HUGE difference in your core temperature to have light colored clothing. A dark colored hat or shirt will cause you to overheat.

Poison ivy is a serious affliction. If you get poison ivy you will be out of the game for 2 weeks. You should be able to identify poison ivy just by looking at it. The leaves are mitten shaped, with a "thumb" that sticks out. LOOK WHERE YOU ARE WALKING. I mean really look. Poison ivy is EVERYWHERE near lakes and rivers. As a general rule, don't touch anything green! Seriously.

You can buy some TECNU and carry it with you in the summer. Tecnu will bind with and remove urushiol, the oil in poison ivy. If you notice yourself brushing against poison ivy, using Tecnu within 20 minutes will keep you from getting the poison ivy rash. If you don't know how to recognize poison ivy, look it up on the internet and become familiar with it.

Insect repellent is a NECESSITY in summer. You will get eaten alive out there without it. I prefer Picaridin based repellents over DEET. Concentrated DEET melts plastics, and DEET has an unpleasant smell. I use 20% concentrated Picaridin, which lasts up to 8 hours. It's best to spray your hand, and then wipe the repellent on your face and neck.

WINTER CONSIDERATIONS

You need 40 degrees and full sun as a minimum, with sustained winds less than 10 mph for winter artifact hunting in the water. Winter floating requires stocking foot neoprene chest waders. DO NOT USE THE OLD STYLE RUBBER WADERS. They will drown you if you fall into fast moving water. Older style rubber waders can billow out from water currents and hold you under. Waders with rubber boots attached are a puncture waiting to happen. Waders with boots attached tend to puncture at the top of the boot where it connects to the waders. Stocking foot waders last much longer and are more comfortable and reliable. You will need an oversized pair of tennis shoes for your neoprene stocking foot waders. Your regular river shoes will not fit over the thick neoprene.

WINTER FLOATING REQUIRES NEOPRENE CHEST WADERS!

When floating, don't forget your dry bag with a change of clothes in case you fall into the water or capsize. Winter floating REQUIRES this backup dry bag. Once you are wet and its 40 degrees out, you can die from exposure in a matter of hours. You might be hours from help when you fall in and get wet, and eventually YOU WILL FALL IN AND GET WET, even if you are careful. It's INEVITABLE. The dry bag should contain a towel for drying yourself, long underwear, a stocking cap, a long sleeve t-shirt, a sweat shirt, pants, and a light windbreaker. Buy a nice DRY BAG made for the purpose of floating, do not use plastic trash bags, they will not keep clothes dry if you capsize. Don't be cheap with your winter gear, YOUR LIFE DEPENDS ON THIS GEAR, literally.

It's possible to walk creeks in the winter with knee high rubber boots. The only problem is these rubber boots are not made for long hikes, and you will get blisters after wearing them on an all-day hike. The best gear is a pair of SEALSKINZ knee high waterproof socks worn with your regular boots or tennis shoes. These socks are expensive, but worth every penny. Leave your jeans down over the socks when walking through the woods, or your socks will get burs all over them. Once you get to the water, tuck your jeans into the top of your waterproof socks so they don't get wet.

Deer Hunting Season: Don't Get Shot!

You need to become familiar with hunting season dates in your area. It is EXTREMELY dangerous to go artifact hunting during hunting season. Turkey season comes before deer season, but most turkey hunters are active in the mornings and are gone by noon. There is an extended hunting season for black powder hunters and bow hunters, but you don't need to worry so much about black powder hunters. They only get one shot and tend to be VERY careful what they shoot at. Bow hunters won't give you too much of a problem, they need to get close to game and don't make many mistakes.

Rifle season is what you should FEAR. Untrained hunters do not bother to identify their targets and shoot anything that moves in the underbrush. Even if you wear a full body suit in hunters orange, you could still take one to the dome if you are hiking the woods during rifle season. DO NOT go hiking around during rifle deer season hunting arrowheads.

However, during rifle season you can dig for artifacts if you have a spot, or you could hunt lake shores without having too much to worry about. Be sure to wear an orange hat. I do not recommend wearing an orange vest. One artifact hunter was wearing an orange vest and drove past a game check station. They chased him down and pulled him over, assuming he was a deer hunter trying to avoid them. He had a difficult time convincing them he wasn't hunting deer.

Remember to CHECK THE WEATHER before you leave the house. Avoid thunderstorms and high winds. It might be warm when you leave the house, but temperatures can go below freezing at night. Bring enough warm clothing to be able to survive overnight in case you get stuck out there for some reason. I carry a lightweight waterproof jacket and pants just in case, you can buy them pretty cheap at any big-box store in the camping section. ALWAYS carry your survival kit, even for short hikes. I prefer using a small backpack for day hikes. Get a nice pack with a waist belt and chest strap. My Columbia backpack has an emergency whistle built into the chest buckle, and large gear pockets on the waist belt.

Chapter 14: When There is No Rain

Nine Ways to Skin a Cat

If you are waiting around for rain, you are missing the big picture. While it's true that rain creates the erosion that uncovers arrowheads and it is important to take advantage of rainstorms, you should NOT be waiting around for rain. There are many methods that do not require rain.

Spillway Hunting-There is the erosional equivalent of a spring flood every day below most dams. Points are released from the same spots EVERY DAY. You can hunt the river banks for many miles below these dams, the daily flood turns over rocks and primes the gravel bars.

Lake Hunting-Wave action on submerged sites knocks loose arrowheads on a regular basis. Camps under 1-3 feet of water are ideal for this type of hunting, even in winter. You can walk these sites wearing chest waders and just look through the water at the bottom, or use your underwater viewer.

Digging-You can dig anytime of the year, rain or drought. I have even dug at night to beat the heat. Hard dry soil can be penetrated if you wet it down first. A five gallon bucket plus a nearby water source and you are in business.

Bank Hunting in Winter-The freeze/thaw cycle in winter is responsible for the bulk of erosion on cut-banks, not flooding or rain. If temperatures drop below freezing at night and then come above freezing during the day, cut-banks are slumping.

Plowed fields-You can hunt plowed fields if the dirt is fresh turned, even without a rain to uncover flint. I have found many nice points in newly plowed dry fields.

Construction sites-These can be surface hunted without any rain, and you might be able to dig if you get permission.

Grubbing-You can go grubbing in the river or lake anytime, no rain necessary.

Drought Hunting-Dropping water levels in times of drought expose new sites on lakes and new gravel bars in the river. Wave action uncovers artifacts, even without rain. Times of drought can be a real boon to the expert arrowhead hunter.

Wild Game and Farm Animals-Animals expose artifacts. I have found many points in cattle tracks near rivers. Gophers digging holes on Indian camps often kick arrowheads out of their dens, leaving them right on the surface fully exposed.

Arrowhead I.T.
Arrowhead Information Technology is the use of computers to discover, retrieve, and manipulate data that helps you recover artifacts.

Knowledge is power; power to find Indian camps and arrowheads. If you aren't good with computers and search engines you won't get far hunting artifacts in the modern world. Computers allow you to develop good leads for Indian camp locations without ever leaving your house.

Construction Sites

Construction permits issued by city and county governments are public information. Check your city and county websites and you can find a list of recently granted construction permits. This list will tell you exactly where and when ALL the construction in your area is taking place! Then go to your online mapping service and pull up a topographic map. Any construction near a river, creek, or spring is worth a closer look. Write up a list of likely spots, and you have an artifact hunting plan. These construction permit lists will even tell you who you need to talk to for hunting permission.

Road and Bridge Projects

Most states maintain a Department of Transportation website that lists road closings and their durations. This is done to help citizens and over-the-road truckers who need to plan alternate routes for their travels. Road and bridge projects are listed with start dates and locations. You want to concentrate on projects near a watercourse of any size. Many modern roads were once animal trails that also acted as highways for ancient man. Indian camps are often located where these old trails (now modern highways) and rivers intersect. This information is often available a year in advance of actual construction.

Hydroelectric Dams

You can check water levels below hydroelectric dams on the United States Geological Survey Real Time Water Data website. Then you know when to schedule a gravel bar hunt on foot or a river bank hunt by kayak. The power company that manages the dam will have their own website and you will find a phone number there to an automated recording. This automated recording will give you planned power generation schedules for today, tomorrow, and the next day. They will tell you one of four options for each day; no generation, light generation, medium generation, and heavy generation. Ideally you want to hunt artifacts on a NO GENERATION day right after a HEAVY GENERATION day.

Lake Information

Many fishing websites on the internet give daily lake level reports as well as temperature information. You can use these websites to learn when lake levels drop during times of drought. If you have previously identified submerged lake sites, you already know the water level at which a particular site is exposed. You can easily plan a lake hunt with this information.

Historical Accounts

You can learn a lot about where Indians lived by reading history. I have found valuable information on county historical society websites. Diaries of early settlers are a gold mine. Reading this information is a good way to get a feeling for the mindset of Indians and how they operated. I have located Indian stone quarries, as well as determined where major trails were located using historical accounts. In some cases there are maps with village locations! Even without an actual map, locations of camps are given in vague but useable terms. For example, you might read "a large encampment of red men once existed at the mouth of Bull Creek." This mouth of a creek is where it flows into a larger river. I have also found paintings of Indian villages that tell where and when they were painted in a caption underneath.

If You Have No Computer

Even without access to a computer you can STILL gather information. Watch your local TV news, and if you see a story about a new running path being dug by the river go check it out. If you see OPEN DIRT anywhere while driving around, double back and check it out. I have seen dump trucks delivering fill dirt to construction sites nowhere near the water. Check the dirt piles; they can have arrowheads in them. Many times the dirt was dug from sites near the river that were once Indian camps. If you find a dump truck pile that produces artifacts, wait around for the dump truck to return. Then follow the dump truck back to where it's being loaded with artifact laden dirt, now you have TWO spots to look!

Windows of opportunity are literally EVERYWHERE and many don't require rain. You are only limited by your imagination, and I have used all the above mentioned information gathering techniques to successfully recover artifacts. This is artifact hunting in the modern world.

Epilogue

"There is more to arrowhead hunting than luck." Willy B.

I am not really after the rocks, although I have learned to appreciate these artworks of ancient man. I love artifact hunting because I love to solve problems. Surface hunting arrowheads is the most difficult task I have encountered. Solving difficult problems with complicated solutions is the ultimate prize for me. Finding Indian artifacts every weekend year round would be impossible, right? Maybe even the hardest problem of all.......Seven years later I am doing just that. Nothing is impossible.

I don't have all the answers. This book is not the complete definition of the Modern School of Artifact Hunting. It's only a beginning. However, as the author of this book, I am your mentor. It is your duty to build on this knowledge and improve it further. By looking inward for answers you realize your full potential, and the student becomes the master.

Happy Hunting,
Willy Bauer

Expert Arrowhead Hunter

ALL COMMENTS AND CORRECTIONS WELCOME
This is my first book, and I am sure it needs work!
Email: willy@wheretofindarrowheads.com